Bernd Weikl

Swastikas on Stage

Bernd Weikl

Swastikas on Stage

Trends in the production of Richard Wagner's operas
in German theaters today

Translated from the German
by Susan Salms-Moss

Bibliographical information published by the
Deutsche Nationalbibliothek (German National Library)
The German National Library catalogues this publication
in the German National Bibliography. Detailed bibliographical data
can found on the Internet at http://dnb.d-db.de.

Bernd Weikl
Swastikas on Stage
Trends in the production of Richard Wagner's operas in German theaters today

Translation: © 2015 Susan Salms-Moss
All rights reserved

Graphics: Horst Thom 2015

Berlin: Pro BUSINESS 2015

ISBN 978-3-86460-305-1

1st edition 2015

Cover: Portrait of Richard Wagner by Franz von Lenbach (1836-1904)

I wish to thank my dear colleague and friend
Susan Salms-Moss for her excellent translation and great
help with the preparation of the manuscript
and my dear Viennese friend Horst Thom for his graphics
that perfectly complement Part VI.
Thanks also to my ally, Attorney Dr. Gerd Rohde,
for his knowledgeable support in legal matters.

Contents

Foreword

January 27, 2015, marked the 70th anniversary of the liberation of Auschwitz. The media reported extensively on this event and on comments made by politicians and some of the 300 remaining survivors. All of them called for efforts against intolerance, indifference and antisemitism. A former prisoner, Roman Kent, said that, were this possible, he would like to add an Eleventh Commandment: "You should never be a bystander."

The German President, Joachim Gauck, has said that throughout his life he has never been able to comprehend the fact that the German nation, blessed with such an honorable culture, had been capable of committing the most monstrous of human crimes. "The society in which we live," said the German President, "will only thrive if the dignity of the individual is respected and solidarity is practiced."[1] It is for this reason that the state educational mandate must be adhered to and freedom of expression and freedom of the press must have certain limitations.

I hope that the contents of this book will open the reader's eyes. Every one of us must demand adherence to the honorable culture referred to by Mr. Gauck, one that leads to altruistic human behavior with the greatest of sensitivity.

And what does Richard Wagner have to do with this?

Wagner's anti-Jewish publications – nota bene, I am not referring to his musical compositions – were primarily mo-

---

[1] Heiner Kiesel, "Gauck: Aus dem Erinnern ergibt sich ein Auftrag." *Die Welt,* January 27, 2015.

tivated by his radical, socially critical ideology. He was aligned with the French utopian socialists, who, among other things, propagated an anti-capitalist hostility toward Jews. From this starting point, he went on to criticize the Jewish mentality, seeing it as a malady of materialism, rather than one based on biological facts. Wagner's point was that the Jews had to be "redeemed." Then they would lose their demonic, destructive power, to be "reborn with us."

Hitler and his followers turned these Wagnerian concepts into the mass murder of millions, an interpretation founded on a terrible misunderstanding. Cosima, of course, was an ingrained antisemite, and her followers obediently supported and expanded this appalling misinterpretation until 1945.

In 2012, I published my first book, *Freispruch für Richard Wagner?*[2] In it, I vainly attempted to somewhat denazify the composer – while not freeing him from blame for his anti-Jewish writings.

The book attracted little notice, and its premise was generally not grasped. Even at the few lectures I held at the Richard Wagner Societies, people repeatedly hurled comments at me regarding Wagner's association with Hitler. At the end of my lecture at the Hochschule für Musik in Hamburg, the organizer of the event went so far as to turn to the members of the audience and suggest that they purchase the latest publication by Jens Malte Fischer[3] instead of mine. In it, Fischer states that the composer's music dramas are filled with antisemitic passages. Furthermore,

---

[2] Bernd Weikl and Peter Bendixen, *Freispruch für Richard Wagner?* (Universitätsverlag Leipzig, 2012).
[3] Jens Malte Fischer, *Richard Wagner und seine Wirkung* (Verlag Paul Zsolnay, Vienna)

he says that Wagner cannot be absolved from his share of the responsibility for the Holocaust, for he had served as an "intellectual precursor" to devastating Nazi policies and had "ennobled a beer cellar ideology and made it socially and culturally acceptable."

In 2014, I thus decided to write a new book, the present one, so that I could describe the progressive destruction of our culture, exemplified by the treatment of Wagner in the message promulgated by the media in 2013 – "Wagner is in Hitler and Hitler is in Wagner." Theodor Adorno, for example, believed that figures in Wagner's works who are spurned are actually caricatures of Jews.[4] Today's stage directors, descendants of that era, evidently think that the primary function of opera is that of provoking the audience with unexpected shocks.

Let me be very clear: I have dedicated much of my artistic life to Richard Wagner's music. The appropriate presentation of his works has the greatest possible meaning to me. I am horrified by the twisted misinterpretations of Wagner's masterpieces too frequently being offered to the public, more and more often falsely indicating to the audience that Wagner had written these works as antisemitic vehicles.

To demonstrate how easily this can be done, I therefore decided to provide some provocative staging suggestions of my own for a number of Wagnerian music dramas, to demonstrate the way these works are being presented to an increasing extent in Germany today. Such productions

---

[4] Theodor W. Adorno, "Versuch über Wagner" in *Die musikalischen Monographien* (Verlag Suhrkamp Berlin, 1952).

must always contain swastikas and indications of Wagner's proximity to Hitler. A prime example was the 2013 production of *Tannhäuser* in Dusseldorf. Indeed, swastikas on the stage can lead to a successful career in German opera houses, no matter what opera is involved.

I will be quoting from the German government's educational mandate and the Basic Law of Germany, its constitution. If adherence to these essential components of German law and German society were being monitored, the judiciary and politicians should have long since voiced prohibitions against such productions of Wagner's works.

My goal is to ignite a protest! It should not be permissible for German theaters, which are heavily subsidized by the state, to do such serious harm. And it should not be possible for the media and authors to voice dangerous assertions confirming false concepts as if they were thoroughly researched scientific conclusions. For if these media and these authors were correct, my beloved Wagner would in fact have to be banned in Germany.

Bernd Weikl

Part I

Witnesses for the prosecution

I can't listen to that much Wagner, you know.
I start to get the urge to conquer Poland.

Woody Allen
Manhattan Murder Mystery

1.1. Introduction

The following reflects the views of renowned academics, well-known journalists, and prominent contemporary witnesses, all of whom have publicly spoken on this topic. Their universally respected expertise should also be considered in the formation of a final opinion.

1.2. Prominent witnesses

DIE ZEIT

Claus Spahn, reviewing a Berlin premiere of *Die Meistersinger von Nürnberg*, wrote: "Who or what is the subject when Hans Sachs, in his problematic closing speech, warns of 'foreign mist with foreign baubles,' and predicts that 'people would no longer know what is German and true if it did not live in the honor of the German Masters?' "[1]

---

[1] Claus Spahn, "Was deutsch und echt," *Die Zeit*, April 16, 1998.

"The performance history of the opera is definitive," Spahn wrote. "The work was claimed without much ado for use by national German chauvinism ... [I]t was the Reichsparteitag opera, the Leni Riefenstahl soundtrack, and the morale-boosting work in the Bayreuth war festivals, ... the German national and festival opera per se, which has at all times sparked debates like no other regarding national identity and nationalistic hubris. How much xenophobia is actually involved when the Town Clerk Sixtus Beckmesser is finally ostracized and cast out by the townspeople ...?"

DIE WELT

"Research on antisemitism leaves no doubt," says Matthias Küntzel, "that Wagner's writings link the animosity toward Jews seen in the Christian centuries with the Holocaust. The composer's concept of 'renewal' left only one perspective open for Jews: extinction. Wagner also invented the murderous term 'Verjudung' (judaization) – and was delighted to hear of the anti-Jewish pogroms in Russia.

Wagner accepted Arthur de Gobineau's philosophy of racial inequality and thus anticipated the National Socialist Nuremberg Laws of 1935 "for the protection of German blood." "Wagner," says Künztel, "was even one of the founding fathers of the antisemitic parties that were formed in the German Reich beginning in 1879. And Wagner was proud of this fact."

Künztel names three additional Wagner researchers whose studies have led them to the same conclusion, as they also find sufficient proof of the composer's antisemitism in his music dramas. Among the authors he names are: Marc A.

Weiner, Paul Lawrence Rose, Barry Millington, Saul Friedländer, Hartmut Zelinsky, Ulrich Drüner, Annette Hein,
Gottfried Wagner and Jens Malte Fischer.[2]

FRANKFURTER ALLGEMEINE ZEITUNG

In 2013, Jens Malte Fischer submitted evidence of hatred
toward Jews in Wagner's music as well. "Prominent witnesses of this are Gustav Mahler and Wagner himself in
his statements about Julius Spielmann, who played Mime
in Vienna." Fischer is astonished that almost no academics
and authors are willing to recognize this fact.[3] Many ana-
lysts have carefully considered which figure is connected
with hatred for Jews, and in what form. Gustav Mahler
and Theodor W. Adorno, for example, as well as the Israeli
historian Saul Friedländer, see the figure of Mime – in the
opera *Siegfried* – as "the quintessence of the Jew." The
storyline thus appropriately woven around Mime makes
him appear to be "the total personification of the Jew," as
he becomes Siegfried's mortal enemy, strives for gold, and
is finally murdered by Siegfried as a result of his dark
plans. Many also see Kundry in *Parsifal* as a Jewish figure,
one who could be redeemed by Parsifal were she to be
baptized. Wagner also put this idea in writing himself.

According to author Saul Friedländer, Wagner's music
dramas were not abused by National Socialism. His work
itself, of its own accord, provides sufficient points of reference and thus lends itself to this possibility. This historian also states: "Wagner remained the most important aes-

---

[2] Matthias Küntzel, "Arien für Arier? Einspruch gegen den Richard Wagner-
Kult," *Die Welt am Sonntag*, April 28, 2013.
[3] Jens Malte Fischer, *Richard Wagner und seine Wirkung* (Vienna, 2013).

thetic figurehead until the end of the Third Reich, referred to repeatedly by Hitler when he mentioned the most significant men in German history."[4]

"The proclamation of German victories or defeats in the war was underscored with music by Wagner. After the disaster in Stalingrad, for example, Siegfried's funeral march from *Götterdämmerung* was played. This music is still used today in war films and the like as associative background music, thus indicating its destructive effect." [4]

Even though Hitler often referred to Wagner's music and mysticism, and mentioned him as an individual, Wagner's antisemitic statements were never included in Hitler's speeches and publications, according to Weiner. "Hitler's and Wagner's ideology, his written statements, and those in his music dramas, were already so identical that the Nazis felt there was no necessity for an additional explanation. At the same time, it must be assumed that Hitler, as a celebrated prophet of the hatred of the Jews, did not want to share this position." [5]

Richard Wagner's music dramas address the Germans' 19th century insecurity and fears of that which was foreign, and especially of "Jewishness." In his antisemitic writings, Wagner as an author repeatedly speaks of a culture that is threatened by the Jews. It is for this reason, according to Marc A. Weiner,[5] that Wagner also applied his criticism in his essay "Jewishness in Music" to his compositions. He created a kind of utopian humanity, a mythical, Germanic,

---

[4] Eleonore Böning, "Jens Malte Fischer: Richard Wagner und seine Wirkung: Ohne Ekstase keine Musikzauberei," *Frankfurter Allgemeine Zeitung,* May 1, 2013.
[5] Marc A. Weiner, *Antisemitische Fantasien* (Berlin, 2000).

or at least Nordic region as an antithesis to the Jewish demon, which is always setting out to destroy that which is noble, pure. The blond, Aryan heroes in Wagner's music dramas bear the names Siegmund, Siegfried, Tristan, Stolzing, Hans Sachs and Parsifal. The dark powers are Ortrud, Kundry, Holländer, Beckmesser, Mime, Hagen, Klingsor and Venus. Wagner already differentiates them in their outer appearance, in their vocal category, and in the vocal music written for them. German, blond, vocally radiant heroes are contrasted with repugnant, devious, destructive, evil figures with their appropriately unappealing external appearance, their unattractive song composed of ungratifying musical structures – see Beckmesser – as caricatures of Jews.

The Ring of the Nibelung presents a political structure that is threatened by foreign powers, evil Jewish caricatures. Siegfried, for example, is the radiant, blond and appealing Teuton, whose side one can take and whom one would want to protect. The horribly unappealing antipodes, these destructive stage figures, are named Beckmesser, Mime, Alberich and Klingsor. They also include the mendacious, evil Ortrud and the immoral ladies Venus and Kundry. Their task is to cause harm to the noble individuals and to the Aryan political entity.

Theodor W. Adorno also believes that Wagnerian antisemitism can be clearly seen and heard in the Nibelung cycle. The gold grubbing, invisible and anonymous, exploitative Alberich, the shrugging, garrulous Mime, brimming over with self-praise and deceit – all of the spurned figures in Wagner's works can be easily recognized as caricatures of Jews. Paul Lawrence Rose provides a similar description in his book *Richard Wagner und der Antisemitismus (Richard*

Wagner and Antisemitism). He says that the greedy Nibe-lung brothers bring to mind "alone through the way they sing ... that which Wagner called 'the Semitic way of speaking' and described in 'Jewishness in Music' as a 'creaking, squeaking, buzzing snuffle.' "[6]

DER SPIEGEL

In 1997, Rudolf Augstein asked in *Der Spiegel* what rela-tionships could be shown between Adolf Hitler, the de-stroyer of the world, and Wagner, the creator of Valhalla. "Do Richard Wagner's music and writings bear guilt for Hitler's atrocities?"[7]

After the German Armed Forces were defeated outside of Moscow in 1942, Hitler is said to have referred to the mys-ticism of his idol. "When I hear Wagner, I have the feeling that these are the rhythms of the primeval world!" Aug-stein quotes Joachim Köhler[8] and Brigitte Hamann[9] to demonstrate the close relationships between the "destroyer of the world" and the "creator of Valhalla." Adolf Hitler thoroughly delved into Wagner's theoretical, antisemitic writings, and undoubtedly also into his apocalyptic vision. According to God's plan, the German race, pure because it is Aryan, is to produce heroes in order to conquer the "grim world anarchy." Following his trial and brief prison sentence in Landsberg, Hitler was at the center of a special antisemitic elite that admired Richard Wagner as its proph-

---

[6] Paul Lawrence Rose, *Richard Wagner und der Antisemitismus* (Zurich, 1999).
[7] Rudolf Augstein, Siegfried, "Lohengrin, Parsifal - Hitler?," *Der Spiegel*, July 21, 1997.
[8] Joachim Köhler, *Wagners Hitler, der Prophet und sein Vollstrecker* (Munich, 1997).
[9] Brigitte Hamann, *Hitlers Wien, Lehrjahre eines Diktators* (Munich, 2012).

et. The Festspielhaus in Bayreuth became a center of this world view, a kind of national shrine. In addition to Wagner's antisemitic writings, the Führer was partial to his music dramas. His secretary reported on Hitler's final wish before his suicide: He wanted to hear "Isoldes Liebestod" from *Tristan und Isolde.*

Hitler identified himself with the figure of Siegfried in *Götterdämmerung* and possibly also with Wotan, the father of the gods, in a world in decline. At the end, he felt that he had been betrayed by the German people, which was not yet mature enough for victory. Hitler saw as many as 140 performances of Wagner's *Götterdämmerung* and other parts of the *Ring des Nibelungen,* which is performed on four evenings, as his secretary reported. However, the homeland betrayed the victorious front – and him as its Führer – in Stalingrad, just as the evil, swarthy Hagen in *Götterdämmerung* ignominiously stabbed the heroic, blond Siegfried from behind. Hitler's most successful speech in Munich spoke of the "stab-in-the-back legend," Germany's defeat in World War One.

He had himself painted as Lohengrin, the Knight of the Grail from the opera with the same name, defender against the "Jewish-Bolshevist invasion of the Mongols" in 1935. And the name "Barbarossa" for his crusade against the Jewish-Asian subhumans was not a pseudonym, but a reference to Kaiser Friedrich I, to whom Wagner originally also intended to dedicate a composition. In 1871, the composer still raved about this "Barbarossa" and described him as a figure of "great, barbaric, sublime, even divine uncertainty." Hitler's Barbarossa began in 1939 with his attack on Russia.

Hitler idealized Cola di Rienzi, the title figure in Wagner's *Rienzi*, making him into a redeemer figure, although he was seen as a failure and was stoned and burned. "At that hour it all began," he told Kubizek, his Vienna school friend, in Bayreuth in 1939, describing his sinister vision. He saw himself as a redeemer and ended his life by suicide. His body was burned. He designed the so-called "Rienzi-Standarten," flags which were ceremoniously dedicated in 1923 at the first Parteitag in Munich and were soon seen everywhere, with the additional phrase "Deutschland erwache" (Germany, awaken) and the swastika. And the overture to *Rienzi* was heard, not only at the Nuremberg Party Rallies.

"This is a shadow in which music and the Holocaust are joined. Wagner's music lies over the Holocaust like a dark cloud. Wagner, the maniacal genius, was not only a composer, but also had an influence on Adolf Hitler and the 'Third Reich,' even though he was already dead by then." No, Wagner was not personally present, but Hitler was able to learn from him. And this is why there was a Wagner in Hitler, and there was also a Hitler in the memory of Wagner.[10]

Journalist Joachim Köhler discusses this explicitly in his 1997 book.[11] Köhler's publisher is very informative regarding the contents: "It is known that Adolf Hitler had been an admirer of Richard Wagner since his earliest youth. What is much less widely known is the extent to which Hitler identified with Wagner's ideology during his lifetime." Joachim Köhler has evaluated all of the available

---

[10] Dirk Kurbjuweit, "Wagners Schatten," *Der Spiegel,* March 30, 2013.
[11] Joachim Köhler, *Wagners Hitler, der Prophet und sein Vollstrecker* (Munich, 1997).

sources and relevant literature and shows us a Hitler who is strongly influenced by Wagner, not only substantively, but also in regard to the dramaturgy and the pomp used in his appearances, his theatricality, his basic rhetorical pattern.

From Richard Wagner's antisemitic, hate-filled rants in "Jewishness in Music," Hitler was able to learn what he could actually put into practice. There the composer invokes the downfall of the Jews, according to Dirk Kurbjuweit in *Der Spiegel.* Köhler detects considerable antisemitism in the operas. "Characters like Mime in *Siegfried* and Kundry in *Parsifal,*" he argues, "are evil caricatures of the supposedly inferior Jews." Köhler finds that *Parsifal* anticipates the racial theories of the Nazis. He quotes Propaganda Minister Joseph Goebbels as follows: "Richard Wagner taught us what the Jew is." According to Köhler, the Green Hill is a hotbed of evil and Wagner the forefather of the Holocaust.

Noah Klieger (86), an Israeli journalist and a survivor of the Holocaust, describes the composer as follows: "Wagner was more than an antisemite. He wanted all Jews to be exterminated." Klieger refers to a letter to Cosima, who had told her husband about the 1881 fire at the Burgtheater in Vienna, in which some 400 people, including a number of Jews, had been killed. Wagner's answer proves his close link to the Holocaust: "All Jews should burn to death at a performance of *Nathan.*"[12]

---

[12] Noah Klieger, "Warum ich Wagner nicht hören will," *Der Spiegel,* July 9, 2012.

"The music of the womanizer and antisemite Richard Wagner is addictive to real fans," said Katja Sembritzki on the occasion of the composer's 200th birthday on May 22, 2013. "This music also inebriated Adolf Hitler. And this is why one ought to ask oneself whether it is permissible to enjoy it if the top Nazi criminal also took delight in it. This all began with Wagner's misanthropic pamphlet "Jewishness in Music," in which he denies that Jews have the ability for musical expression, and in which, for purposes of argumentation, he becomes one of the first to change from a religiously motivated hatred of Jews to early racist antisemitism. In light of this, it seems problematic for Wagner enthusiasts to brush this inflammatory publication aside as a mere foible in order to prevent any suspicion from falling on the musical works of the composer. The Ride of the Valkyries from *Der Ring des Nibelungen* was used as background music for successful German air raids in Nazi newsreels, and *Die Meistersinger von Nürnberg* was regularly performed at party rallies.

In his collection of essays *Richard Wagner und seine Wirkung* (Richard Wagner and his Effect), cultural scientist Jens Malte Fischer not only shows that the National Socialists seized upon concrete approaches in Wagner's writings and further developed them, but also documents signs of antisemitism in the characterization of certain figures in Wagner's music dramas and the way they sing. "Today's audience would no longer comprehend these suggestions, but Wagner's contemporaries would most certainly have understood the innuendos." The antisemitic pamphlet "Jewishness in Music" had "fatal consequences," because it finally made antisemitism truly socially acceptable, having gained considerably in acceptability due to this widely admired artist."[13]

LEIPZIG

The new Wagner monument was unveiled in Leipzig on May 22, 2013, to mark the 200th birthday of the composer. Burkhard Jung, the Mayor of Leipzig, was of the opinion that the city did not need this monument.[14] What compelled the city to erect it? Wagner was not an honorary citizen of Leipzig. In fact, he was actually not from Leipzig at all, but from Stötteritz, a village that had been incorporated only a hundred years earlier. And until recently, the composer's music dramas had not even been on the program in the Leipzig opera house.

An exhibition at the Leipzig Museum of City History is dedicated to him. It rightly disassociates itself from the antisemitic composer through its title – "Wagner. Pleasure and Pain." The curators let Thomas Mann speak: "It is a ghastly feeling to know how much, with the character of an abominable petit bourgeois, he (Wagner) actually anticipates National Socialism ...." They also quote the conductor Simon Rattle, who states: "The more I read about Wagner, the more difficult I find it to perform his music." And Thomas Mann says again, in 1940: "I see the Nazi element not only in Wagner's questionable literature; I see it in his music, too." In 1940, this important author also finds that Wagner's music dramas have their origins in the bourgeois humanistic epoch, just as Hitlerism does. Then

---

[13] Katja Sembritzki, "Schützenjäger, Antisemit, begnadeter Komponist. Wagners dunkle Flecken bleiben," *ntv.de*, May 22, 2013.
[14] Barbara Möller, "Warum Leipzig sein Richard Wagner-Denkmal nicht liebt," *Die Welt*, May 15, 2013.

Mann criticizes the "Wagala weia" of the composer, his mixture of tradition and future, and the alliterations he uses in his text. Mann sees Wagner's concept of a reborn, classless society as the intellectual basis for National Socialism. This mythical reactionary revolutionism leads directly to Hitler.[15] "There is a great deal of Hitler in Wagner," wrote Thomas Mann.[16]

MUNICH

In the summer of 2012, the Bavarian State Opera produced a fringe program for the *Ring des Nibelungen* on the Jakobsplatz in Munich. The discussion revolving around the presentation of Wagner's music dramas in Israel was treated theatrically. Under the title "Hacking Wagner," the organizers planned to repeat this on November 19, 2013, at the Munich Jewish Center and announced the concert as follows: "Richard Wagner/Brilliant Composer/and Antisemite/A Provocation." The plan was to use the antisemitic parts of Wagner's written communications in printed form, to be read or played as video messages, and juxtapose them with the "Siegfried Idyll." The concert had to be cancelled, as it was considered to be politically incorrect. "One can only hope that there will soon be an opportunity to judge oneself whether music is perceived in a different way if one is simultaneously confronted with his an-

---

[15] Thomas Mann, "Zu Wagners Verteidigung," *Leiden und Größe der Meister,* (Frankfurt am Main, 1959).
[16] Hans R. Vaget, *Im Schatten Wagners: Thomas Mann über Richard Wagner* (Frankfurt am Main, 2010).

tisemitic tirades with the help of various media," suggests Klaus Kalchschmid.[17]

DER NORDBAYERISCHE KURIER

In the *Nordbayerischer Kurier* of October 31, 2013, Jens Malte Fischer discusses the effect of Wagner's antisemitic statements on Adolf Hitler. "At least a hundred of the most vicious antisemitic remarks can be found in Cosima's diaries, which clearly prove how the composer's malicious attitudes toward the Jews became even worse as he aged. Hitler had even used the same choice of words in his bible, *Mein Kampf,* thus clearly showing to what extent the Führer had copied Wagner." "The question," says Fischer, "as to whether there are indications of Jewishness in Wagner's operas, such as in characters like Mime and Beckmesser, must be increasingly answered with 'yes' – particularly this year (2013)."[18] "Hitler regarded Richard Wagner as "the greatest prophet the German people had, and therefore as his only idol. He compared 'his Kampf' with the difficult situations Wagner had to endure during most of his life."[19]

If Wagner posed the question as to whether it might be possible at some time to hinder the decline of "our culture" by violently casting out the subversive foreign elements (the Jews) with the help of powers not yet known by him, Hitler must have been familiar with this statement. In any case, he and his followers acted in line with it and

---

[17] Klaus Kalchschmid, "Wagner und der Antisemitismus," *Süddeutsche Zeitung,* November 15, 2013.
[18] Jens Malte Fischer, *Richard Wagner und seine Wirkung* (Vienna, 2013).
[19] Joachim Fest, *Hitler, eine Biografie* (Berlin, 1998).

murdered millions of Jews.[20] The contents of Wagner's hate-filled writings and, explicitly, his antisemitic music dramas, as well, were passed on to Goebbels and others by his widow Cosima, his son-in-law Chamberlain, Alfred Rosenberg, and his daughter-in-law Winifred. As a reminder: Wagner differentiated clearly between non-Jews and Jews. He compared the latter – as already mentioned, as destined by nature – with "worms," "rats," "mice," "warts" or "parasites."[21] In 1881, he wrote to King Ludwig II: "… [I] believe … the Jewish race is the born enemy of pure humanity and everything noble in it." Through this statement alone, Wagner became the source of Hitler's ideas for his Nuremberg Reichstag speech of January 30, 1939, and the Holocaust.

For decades, most of the programs for performances of Wagner's music dramas in opera houses in Germany have mentioned the composer's antisemitism. This applies as well to reviews in the media for these productions, which unanimously refer to Wagner's murderous hatred for the Jews. In the theater and music departments of the universities in Germany and Austria, Richard Wagner's antisemitism has a regular place in the curriculum. Students who have reflected this in their written work often take up posts in opera houses and in the media once they have earned their degrees.

In this context, it is stressed again and again – but unfortunately in vain up to the present – that this topic needs to

---

[20] Joachim Köhler, *Wagners Hitler*, der Prophet und sein Vollstrecker (Munich, 1997).
[21] Matthias Küntzel, "Arien für Arier? Einspruch gegen den Wagnerkult," Welt am Sonntag, April 28, 2013.

be dealt with urgently. All such efforts are also supported by the state and the regional media. (Examples: Kulturstiftung des Bundes, Zeit-Stiftung Ebelin und Gerd Bucerius, Friede Springer Stiftung, Oberfrankenstiftung, City of Bayreuth, Stiftung der Bayerischen Wirtschaft, etc.) In the final analysis, however, successful processing could only occur if charges were brought and the guilty party, or his music dramas, were condemned. Richard Wagner's great-grandson has been demanding this for years.

Gottfried Wagner stated this again authentically in 2013 and was taken very seriously by the most important video, audio and print media in Germany. The composer, his great-grandfather, is explicitly mentioned everywhere in the same breath as Hitler. Richard Wagner is shown to be the first in a series of people that continued with Cosima Wagner, Houston Chamberlain, Ernst Alfred Rosenberg, Himmler, Göring, Goebbels, Eichmann, many other Nazis, and naturally Hitler. The extremely dangerous psychological effect of Wagner's music can no longer be permitted, he claims, and therefore wrote: *You Shall Have No Other Gods Before Me. Richard Wagner – A Minefield.*

Wagner's great-grandson demands an end to the Wagner cult. He wants to settle a score. His publisher's advertising text reads: "2013 is a Wagner jubilee year. In the idyllic world of the Wagnerians, everyone agrees: The legend must be fostered, Bayreuth maintained as a cult site and place of pilgrimage. Critical questions regarding the ideology of the celebrated titan or how close his descendants were to the Nazis are to be swept under the red carpet. Richard's great-grandson Gottfried, the son of Wolfgang Wagner, who was the director of the Festspiele for many years, has raised his voice against this phalanx of disciples.

As a music historian, he has spent his life dealing critically with the life, work and ideology of his ancestor. Now he had produced a paper countering unashamed and irresponsible adherence to the Wagner legend. Gottfried Wagner has appealed again and again for a critical examination of the dark side of the family history, opening of the archives, and scrutinizing of the Wagner cult. But the keepers of the Bayreuth Grail lack any serious such volition, even under the aegis of sisters Katharina and Eva. In sharp contrast to the jubilee homage, Gottfried demonstrates his grandfather's true nature: that of an antisemite, misogynist, and disdainer of life, driven by self-idolatry and a yearning for death. He refers to the close connection between Wagner's delusional ideas and the psychological effect of his music and settles his score with all those who close their eyes to this dangerous side of their idol and deny the connection between his ideology, his life, and the creation of his operas. This is a political and cultural polemic paper of the greatest explosiveness and topicality."[22]

Gottfried Wagner was praised by the media for this book: "More than a retaliation. A counterpoint to the chorus of glory and honor. Radical ... authentic."[23] "As exciting to read as a thriller, and it brings a breath of fresh air into the Wagner year."[24] "Vehement voice against the cheers of jubilation."[25]

---

[22] Gottfried Wagner, *Du sollst keine anderen Götter haben neben mir: Richard Wagner – Ein Minenfeld* (Berlin, 2013).

[23] Wolfgang Schreiber, "Gottfried Wagner: Du sollst keine anderen Götter haben neben mir," *Süddeutsche Zeitung*, April 20, 2013.

[24] Ulla Zierau, "Kulturgespräch: Misstöne im Jubeljahr," *SWR2, May 3, 2013.*

[25] "Vehemente Gegenstimme zu den Jubelarien," *Neue Presse*, Ullstein Buchverlage, *April 27, 2013*

Part II

Antisemitic writings
and statements on record

Since 1945, renowned authors and journalists have been meeting at symposiums in Germany at regular intervals to exchange their views on what seems to be the constantly increasing antisemitism of Richard Wagner. It is interesting to note that hardly any speakers with differing views of the composer seem to be invited. So these symposiums are more or less closed societies. The results of such meetings serve in Part II as the basis for the "brown thread" of antisemitic attitudes that progressed from Richard Wagner and his widow to the Holocaust of the Nazis. However, it is essential for us to differentiate between the composer's antisemitic writings, Cosima's "second hand" statements, the interpretations of the Hitler regime, and the treatments – and assumptions – of present-day authors and journalists.

2.1. Introduction

How did Richard Wagner's writings and works influence Adolf Hitler (1889-1945) personally? Were the gestures and rhetoric he used in his public appearances not in fact inspired by Wagner's characters?

Joseph Goebbels (1897-1945) lauded Hitler's "Kunst der Massenführung" (art of mass leadership) in 1936 in similarly effusive words: It is "... so unique and distinctive that it doesn't fit any scheme or dogma. It would be absurd to imagine that he might have attended some kind of school for speakers or orators. He is a genius in the art of rhetoric, one who has developed on his own, without help from anyone else, least of all consciously."[1]

On the other hand, Bertolt Brecht (1898-1951) said in 1941 that he thought the "Führer" had taken instruction in declamation and performance from a minor actor named Basil. In his allegory *The Resistible Rise of Arturo Ui,* the main character and mobster boss — and none other than Adolf Hitler is meant here — is thoroughly trained to become a stage actor.[2] Involved here are facial expressions and gestures, walking, standing, or folding his arms in front of his chest — used in order to ultimately impress the masses.

In reality, Adolf Hitler did in fact have a teacher. The renowned opera singer Paul Stieber-Walter (1890-1973), known as Paul Devrient — he stems from the famed Berlin actor dynasty with the same name — accompanied the "Führer" for many years on his campaign tours. He taught him gestures and trained his rhetoric, just as was needed by Wagner's stage figures and as was so familiar to him as a Wagner singer.[3]

So it was not only Richard Wagner's writings and his music dramas, but also Wagner's image of a hero, leader (Führer) and savior of his people that affected Hitler's personality, his murderous actions, and his diabolical influence on the masses.

---

[1] Adolf Hitler, *Bilder aus dem Leben des Führers* (Altona/Bahrenfeld, 1936).
[2] Bertold Brecht, *Der aufhaltsame Aufstieg der Arturo Ui* (Berlin, 1973).
[3] Paul Devrient, *Mein Schüler Adolf Hitler.* (Munich, 2003).

2.2. Richard Wagner

Hitler was able to learn from Wagner …
There was also some Wagner in Hitler …
So there was also some Hitler in Wagner.[4]

Richard Wagner was born near Leipzig on May 22, 1813. On February 13, 1883, as befitting his social status, he temporarily departed from this earth at the Palazzo Vendramin in Venice – to then graciously bestow his presence on Germany once more in 1889 as Adolf Hitler.

A number of highly influential doctrines, including those of a long succession of prominent thinkers and artists, could be noted as philosophical and ideological companions to Wagner's rebirth. One might mention here, for example, Arthur Schopenhauer (1788-1860) or Ludwig Feuerbach (1804-1872). For Richard Wagner integrated a wealth of suggestions, core elements, and fundamental building blocks drawn from their philosophies in his way of thinking and combined them with the philosophical teachings he found, for example, in Burnouf's *Introduction à l'histoire du Buddhisme indien*[5] (Introduction to the History of Indian Buddhism*)*. No matter how, he was certain that all of these religious and philosophical ideas and programs would prove to be correct.

But definitive topics, such as Feuerbach's antisemitism, must have also met with Wagner's approval, with statements like: "The principle of the Jewish religion is egoism. The Jew is indifferent to everything that is not directly re-

---

[4] Dirk Kurbjuweit, "Wagners Schatten," *Der Spiegel,* No. 14, March 30, 2013.
[5] Renate Wiggerhaus and Ulrike Helmer, Ed., *Malwida Meysenbug, Memoiren einer Idealistin* (Königstein, 1998).

lated to the well-being of his own person. Hebrew egoism is of inscrutable depth and power. The Jews received from Jehovah clemency for stealing ...."[6]

Additional examples can be found.

That Richard Wagner became Adolf Hitler when he was reborn in 1889 was confirmed in 2013 – 200 years after his first birth and 130 years after his first death – in all the serious media and on many pages in newly published books during the Wagner anniversary year: "Wagner is in Hitler, and Hitler is thus also in Wagner," as was researched, summarized, and reported by the media nationally and in part even worldwide.

Jens Malte Fischer, for example, argues with commendable clarity in the following excerpts from the composer's "Jewishness in Music" (published in 1850 and again in 1869) that leave no doubt as to his antisemitism: "A language, with its expression and its evolution, is not the work of individuals, but that of a historical community. Only he who has unconsciously grown up within this community can also take part in that which it creates. The Jew, however, has stood outside any such community, alone with his Jehovah in a fragmented tribe without a land, one to which all self-sprung evolution must be denied, just as even the peculiar (Hebraic) language of that tribe has been preserved for him merely as a thing defunct. To write true poetry in a foreign tongue has remained impossible up to the present, even to the greatest of geniuses. In this language, this art, the Jew cannot truly create a poem or a work of art ....

---

[6] Ludwig Feuerbach, *Das Wesen des Christentums* (Ditzingen, 1984).

"No art offers such a wealthy abundance of opportunities to express something, without actually saying anything concrete, as does music, because the greatest geniuses have already communicated what could be said in it as an absolutely special form of art. Once this had been done, it could only be repeated, word for word and with deceptive similarity, just as parrots imitate human words and speech, but also without expression and true feeling, just like these zany birds ....

"As long as music as a special art has had a real organic need for life, apart from the epochs of Mozart and Beethoven, a Jewish composer was not to be found anywhere. It has been impossible for an element that was entirely foreign to that living organism to take part in the culture of this life. It is only when a body's inner death is apparent that the external elements gain power over it – but merely to destroy it. Then, however, that body's flesh decomposes into a teeming colony of worms. But who, at this sight, would believe that body to still be alive? The spirit, that is, life, has fled from that body to other kindred bodies, and this is the essence of life itself. It is only in true life that we, too, can rediscover the spirit of art, not within its cadaver, eaten away by worms .... For I am certain about one thing: The influence the Jews have gained over our intellectual life, and the way in which it is manifested by distracting from and falsifying our highest cultural tendencies, is not a simple, merely physiological coincidence. It must be recognized as undeniable and decisive."[7] From this, Richard

---

[7] Jens Malte Fischer, *Richard Wagners "Das Judentum in der Musik"* (Frankfurt am Main, 2000).

Wagner draws the conclusion that only their "Untergang" – their downfall – could redeem the Jews.

Wagner had made several comments against the Jews in this particular context. To begin with, there was the above-mentioned pamphlet of 1850 and, in 1869, an open letter to the pianist Marie Muchanoff (1840-1877) entitled "Some Explanations Concerning 'Jewishness in Music'" and a reprint of this essay. Then Wagner wrote two more small treatises for the *Bayreuther Blätter*, which he had founded in 1878, as well as a later version of his extensive essay on "Religion and Art" (1880) and another brief anti-semitic piece about Jews with the title: "Know Thyself" (1881).

The Jew is stylized there as a "plastic demon of humanity's downfall." In 1865, Wagner published a piece in the *Bayreuther Zeitschrift* that dealt with German art and German politics and considered the question of 1867-68: "What is German?" "Modern" *(1878)* was a definite rejection of Judaism by Wagner and Rabbi Friedmann, who pleaded in favor of a "modern" world, as opposed to the old, ortho-dox one.

Finally, Richard Wagner encountered one of the most im-portant theoreticians of modern racism, the Frenchman Arthur de Gobineau (1816-1882), and delved into his racial ideology. His "Essai sur l'inégalité des races humaines" (Essay on the inequality of the human races) was published between 1853 and 1855. Gobineau's pseudoscientific stud-ies were partially based on exterior characteristics like skull form, skin color, physical stature, intelligence and social behavior. This "racial theory" had an unusually great influ-ence on the practice of National Socialism in its attempt to differentiate between Aryans and Jews, members of that "inferior" race. Gobineau was convinced that most of the "races" were not capable of cultivating themselves by their own means.

Seizing upon this, Wagner considered the Jews to be among these. By contrast, he spoke of a "noble race," from which everything on earth emanated "that had to do with human creation, science, art, civilization, that which is great, noble, fruitful." That this meant Aryans, who also supposedly possessed a "special blood that promoted culture," did not have to be specifically mentioned.

Such thought on Wagner's part corresponds with his antisemitic statements in "Jewishness in Music," as well as the idea that dispositions that can be passed on genetically equip their proprietor with a "monopoly of beauty, intelligence and strength," and thus a societal supremacy. A "mixing of the races," on the other hand – as one reads in Gobineau – would be "disastrous."[8] The Nazis called this racial defilement and prosecuted infringements with severe sentences.

"The Jews' overall thoughts and aspirations," wrote Hans A. Grunsky in 1920, "matured apart from occidental and German development,"[9] thus confirming Wagner's observations. The composer's criticism of this race in "Jewishness in Music" applied not only to the sphere of music. After all, no one would have succumbed to the idea of constraining the Jews in a ghetto for centuries if they had

---

[8] Mario Wenzel, "Germanische Herrenrasse," in Wolfgang Benz, Ed., *Handbuch des Antisemitismus. Judenfeindschaft in Geschichte und Gegenwart*, Vol. 3 (Berlin, 2010).
[9] Karl Grunsky, *Richard Wagner und die Juden, Vol. II* (Munich, 1920).

fulfilled their responsibilities as respectable and hard-working citizens. And if the Jews had foregone usury (the banking sector) after they were freed (from the ghetto), it would still have been possible for them to return to real work. "Instead, however," argues Hans A. Grunsky, "when the Jew was freed from the ghetto, he ruthlessly chose the job of an 'art goods trader' (art dealer, theatre agent, etc.) Or, in other words, the European creates something, and the Jew does business with it."

"The Jew has never had art of his own, therefore he has never had a life with artistic content," as Grunsky freely quotes Wagner. "Each people has its talent: the Aryans for art, the Semites for business. We wouldn't change this. But we do ask for one thing: The Jews should leave us in peace to create and not someday think of robbing the art world a second time." Wagner summarizes his thoughts on the Jews' inability to originate any true culture in "Know Thyself" (1881) with the comment that the Jewish instinct bars any ideality.

Wagner's explicitly antisemitic comments are thus manifest in his writings, and anyone has access to Wagner as an author. Just the same, there was a considerable discrepancy between Wagner's clearly negative philosophical position toward Jews and his interactions with Jews on an individual, personal level – which admittedly varied in accordance with existing professional animosities, such as that in connection with Meyerbeer. His friendship with the Jewish conductor Hermann Levi, the son of a rabbi, however, was particularly striking.

On April 27, 1870, for example, Wagner wrote an enthusiastic letter to Levi, saying how pleased he was that he had heard how superbly he had conducted *Die Meistersinger* in Karlsruhe. "I hardly need to tell you how reassuring it is for me to know that a man with real talent is the conductor of a German opera theater. With the utmost respect, Richard Wagner."[10]

Wagner is unambiguous in his comments to Levi. "If I write about Jews again, I would say that I have nothing against them, that they merely came to us Germans too early, and that we were not yet strong enough to absorb this element."[11]

Levi wrote in a letter to his father, Chief Rabbi Dr. Levi in Giessen: "He – Wagner – is the best and noblest person. It is natural that the world around him misunderstands him and maligns him ... Goethe did not fare any better. But posterity will later recognize that Wagner was as great a human being as he was an artist, as those close to him already know. Even his struggle against that which he calls "Jewishness" in music and in modern literature arises from the noblest of motives, and the fact that he harbors no petty *risches* (antisemitism) ... is proven by the way he acts toward me, toward Josef Rubinstein, and by his former personal relationship with Tausig, whom he dearly loved."

When Wagner dies in 1883, Levi is one of his pall bearers. He energetically supports a continuation of the Festspiele under the leadership of Cosima Wagner and continues to conduct his *Parsifal* there. But the "Clique of the Radicals," to which he now belongs as a member of the innermost Wagner circle, does everything possible to make his

---

[10] Erich Kloss, *Richard Wagner an Freunde und Zeitgenossen* (Leipzig and Berlin, 1911).
[11] Hans von Wolzogen, *Bayreuther Blätter 1937* (Bayreuth, 1937).

membership increasingly difficult. In 1888, Levi is missing from Bayreuth for the first time. In 1894, he gives up.

2.3. Cosima Wagner, Houston Stewart Chamberlain, Alfred Rosenberg, Winifred Wagner, Joseph Goebbels, Adolf Hitler

Following Richard Wagner's death in early 1883, his widow Cosima (1837-1930) took command on the "Green Hill" in Bayreuth and established the "völkisch-national" (populist-nationalist) ideology and identity to combat any "foreign proliferation (Jews) that would undermine our entire species." Those governing the country, as the justification read, no longer knew "… that cultures are the product of races. Humane attitudes and speeches would be of no use, for the facts speak a cruel language." Cosima continues: "We now have a German Reich with a Jewish nation," but it is urgently necessary to have a German theater without Jews:[12] "[W]e want a German theater with all nations, with the exception of the 'chosen.' " The "chosen" meant the Jewish artists.[13] Cosima already demonstrated her antisemitic casting policy in her Jew-free *Meistersinger* production in Bayreuth in 1888.

Houston Stewart Chamberlain (1855-1927), born to wealthy, English nobility, was able to lead a fairly carefree existence, due to a lifetime annuity. Interested in literature and music, he was drawn to the writings and works of

---

[12] Hannes Heer, Jürgen Kesting and Peter Schmidt, *Verstummte Stimmen. Die Bayreuther Festspiele und die "Juden" 1876-1945* (Berlin, 2012).
[13] Hannes Heer, Cosima Wagner to Julius Kniese on Oct. 13, 1892, in *Verstummte Stimmen* (Berlin, 1934).

Richard Wagner very early on. In 1882, he attended the Bayreuth Festival and heard, among other works, the world premiere of *Parsifal*. Chamberlain published essays on *Lohengrin* and *Tristan und Isolde* in the Paris *Revue Wagnérienne* and, in May 1888, in the *Sächsische Landeszeitung* in Dresden. "Künstlerische Dankbarkeit" (Artistic Gratitude) was the title of an essay on Wagner's relationship with Franz Liszt. This sparked Cosima's interest in making Chamberlain's acquaintance. They first met on June 12, 1888, at the home of the sculptor Gustav Kietz in Dresden. This was followed by an intensive exchange of letters, in which Cosima and Chamberlain soon revealed themselves to be marked antisemites.

Cosima wrote to Chamberlain on February 8, 1893: "Most recently, I have heard so much about the systematic practice of intermarriage…. [I]f we should soon have to say 'Finis Germaniae,' then we would want to do so with conscious knowledge of the reasons for this downfall." On November 19, 1894, Chamberlain reacted to a letter from Cosima, with the words: "… with how much gratitude I welcome every idea I hardly need to say. Therefore my heartfelt thanks, too, for today's comments regarding Gobineau. Up to now, I had not considered the race question in connection with politics, only with regeneration, then a second time with Gobineau's special emphasis under IV.2 (the Bayreuth thought). In politics, great attention would naturally have to be placed on 'What is German?' but it would have to be more palpable, political and practical." Cosima answered immediately: "At the moment when I included race with politics, I sensed the misdirection. You are absolutely right. And I only wanted to bring up the topic again because the initiative has been taken here, too, and an impetus to the movement has been provided."[14]

In 1896, Chamberlain published a book about Richard Wagner's writings and teachings. In it, he agrees with the composer's thesis that the reason for the misery in the current social condition is money, because money always devalues people. In "Das Kunstwerk der Zukunft" (The Artwork of the Future), he says, Wagner had searched for the source of this downfall, in which the German tribes had totally alienated themselves, and found that this was solely due to the negative moral influence of the Jews and thus the perdition of pure German blood – ideas that later provided grist for the mill of National Socialism.[15]

On February 24, 1898, a letter from Chamberlain to Cosima contained the following: "[W]hen your letter arrived, I was just finishing writing the end of the last insert for the chapter I had completed on Sunday: The arrival of the Jews in Western history. ... I had simply asked myself the question: What is a Jew? ... At the very beginning, I had offered a solemn sacrifice. It is in your power to make a more solemn 'burnt offering' out of it ... [I] would also like to ask you for ideas for my 'Entrance of the Teutons into the History of the World.' ... And now I will close; but since six volumes of the Talmud are lying before me, I would still like to offer a fitting quotation: 'A man should not rear a dog, unless he is bound to a chain.' These few words define the entire ideology."

---

[14] Paul Pretzsch, *Cosima Wagner und Houston Stewart Chamberlain im Briefwechsel, 1888-1908* (Leipzig, 1934).

[15] Houston Stewart Chamberlain, *Richard Wagners Schriften und Lehren* (Munich, 1919).

Cosima answered on May 25, 1899, in reference to *Die Grundlagen des 19. Jahrhunderts (The Foundations of the 19th Century)*: "Your book will last ... and will constitute a new landmark. You are the first person who has the boldness to speak the truth, namely that the Jew plays a significant role in our present culture and that for that reason one must closely study who he is. Wolzogen (1855-1934)[16] said so nicely: Up to now, we thought we knew our Bible stories well, but now it turns out that we didn't know anything at all. 'That the sons preserve their pure blood, but the daughters, on the other hand, mix themselves with us' describes the entire present situation." [Wollzogen had formulated an election appeal for Hitler in the *Völkischer Beobachter* and in it described Hitler as "the candidate for the German intellectual world."]

Chamberlain wrote to Cosima on November 5, 1901: "The real law of our world is that one should never even utter the word 'Jew.' Years ago, in a Strauss operetta, I heard a very lively refrain set to vivid music: 'There are no more men!' In the same way and with equal justification, one can say today: 'There are no more Jews!' And yet these people control everything, even the antisemitic parties."

Cosima Wagner wrote to Chamberlain on February 15, 1902: "Your *Foundations* is the most frequently read book in all layers of society. When we met with His Majesty [Wilhelm II], the Kaiser repeatedly said: 'Chamberlain thinks so, too.' You have come to have a most significant effect, my friend. I am very happy for you about this and

---

[16] Ernst Klee, *Das Personenlexikon zum Dritten Reich: War war was vor und nach 1945* (Frankfurt am Main, 2007).

expect that only good things will come of it."[17] Cosima is alluding here to the fact that Houston Stewart Chamberlain had published *The Foundations of the 19th Century* in 1899 and in it commented that it was of the essence to free the Reich from the crushing grasp of the Jews.

For the Jews have only one objective: world domination. They are diabolical, demonic, and determined to infiltrate other societies in order to subvert that society's pure blood. The Jew invades a society, storms all of the positions, and imposes himself on it. This would make the Germans into a degenerate people and slaves of the Jews.[18]

Chamberlain sent a copy of the book to Kaiser Wilhelm II. The latter answered enthusiastically, saying that, with a stroke of magic, Chamberlain had managed to bring order into the muddle of his Germanic intuitions and pointed out clear paths that should be followed for the good of the Germans and thus for the good of humanity. Wilhelm II bestowed the Iron Cross on Chamberlain and extended an enthusiastic invitation to call on him.

Especially under Chamberlain's influence, Wilhelm's anti-semitic convictions were becoming increasingly intense. Susan Townley told of a conversation with him in which he denounced the Jews as a "curse" for Germany: "Sitting in every little village in Germany is a dirty Jew who draws the people into the net of usury like a spider. He loans money to the small farmers and demands their land as a bond. Thus he gradually gains control over everything. The

[17] Paul Pretzsch, *Cosima Wagner und Houston Stewart Chamberlain im Briefwechsel, 1888-1908* (Leipzig, 1934).
[18] Houston Stewart Chamberlain, *Die Grundlagen des 19. Jahrhunderts* (Munich, 1942).

Jews are the parasites of my empire. The Jewish question is one of my greatest problems, and yet nothing can be done to solve it."

This anti-Jewish attitude on the part of Wilhelm II is demonstrated by a multiplicity of other statements and letters, these later dealing to a greater extent with the apparent solution. A "regular international universal pogrom à la Russe" as the "best remedy" was one of his phantasies during the final years of his life. In the summer of 1929, he wrote: "Jews and mosquitos" are "a plague from which humanity must free itself, no matter how." And he added in his own handwriting: "I think gas would be best."[19]

Returning to Cosima Wagner's correspondence with Chamberlain, she wrote on November 9, 1902: "I read your introduction to the IVth edition of the *Foundations* and find it so outstanding that I cannot resist expressing my thanks to you for it .... Eminent, for example, is your mention of the Jews in regard to the sense of race seen as religion, and that this should be seen as one of the most important moments in our cultural development. One must have it in his blood and, especially, see it. If I wanted to mention all of the examples of the demise of the Germans in the mixture that I myself have seen – I couldn't even manage."

She received an answer only two days later: "[I]f we can finally rid ourselves of Jehovah with your help, I firmly believe that everything will be in order."[20]

---

[19] Bernd Weikl and Peter Bendixen, *Freispruch für Richard Wagner?* (Leipzig, 2012).

[20] Paul Pretzsch, *Cosima Wagner und Houston Stewart Chamberlain im Briefwechsel, 1888-1908* (Leipzig, 1934).

Houston Stewart Chamberlain became Cosima's son-in-law on December 27, 1908. He married Eva Wagner, and the couple moved into the house at Wahnfried Strasse 1 – now the Jean Paul Museum – very close to Cosima's domicile.

Chamberlain was granted German citizenship in August 1916, and in 1917 he became a member of the German Fatherland Party. Chamberlain blamed Germany's defeat in the First World War on the Jews. He also saw his antisemitic racial ideology as a progression of Wagner's conclusions, which ultimately provided the groundwork for the extermination mania of the Nazis. As Chamberlain was barely able to leave his sickbed due to a mercury poisoning, Hitler – on whom he already pinned his hopes – visited him as early as 1923 on Wahnfried Strasse in Bayreuth.

A new group started to develop: "You are not at all the fanatic you have been described to me to be," wrote Chamberlain to his guest under the impact of this encounter. "A fanatic inflames the spirit, but you warm the heart. A fanatic wants to overpower people with words. You only want to convince, and this is the reason you are successful."[21]

Winifred Wagner (1897-1980) was born as Winifred Marjorie Williams in England. Following the early death of her parents, custody was assumed by a couple named Klindworth. Her adoptive father, Karl Klindworth (1830-1916), an admirer of Wagner, wrote the piano scores to some of

---

[21] Wanda Kampmann, *Deutsche und Juden. Studien zur Geschichte des deutschen Judentums* (Heidelberg, 1963).

his works, among other things. He introduced Winifred Williams to the Wagner family, especially to Cosima.

In September 1915, Marjorie Williams married Cosima's son Siegfried Wagner (1869-1930). The bridegroom was 47, the bride all of 18 years old. Four children resulted from this union. Cosima Wagner, who liked to be addressed as "verehrte Meisterin" (revered mistress) at the time and who had become the uncompromising defender of the composer's legacy since his death, was satisfied with her son's marriage: "... [I] sometimes think I am dreaming when I see a comely, youthful being at his side who, reared superbly by our friends, the Klindworths, possesses all of the characteristics that agree with Siegfried's being and harmonize with our home. This is thus a great good fortune, one for which I thank the heavens every day."

Winifred Wagner became a close personal friend of Adolf Hitler, whom she met in 1923 in Bayreuth shortly after the "German Days," and ushered into the family. Although his visit, as already mentioned, had primarily been intended for Chamberlain, he had now become part of the whole Wagner family, and they immediately allied themselves with him. Winifred called him the familiar "Du" as of 1925, and for the four children he was only "Uncle Wolf" from then on.

Daniela Thode (1860-1940), the Chamberlains, and Winifred Wagner (NSDAP Membership No. 29,349) joined the party in 1926. Only Siegfried held off – out of consideration for the Festspiele, for which donations from wealthy Jews were always welcome.[22] Winifred was now working for the family, for the organization of the Festspiele, and for Hitler. And Cosima was deteriorating in a darkened room in Haus Wahnfried, protected by Daniela and Eva as if she were a living monument. She died on April 1, 1930.

After the failed march on the Feldherrnhalle (Beer Hall Putsch) in Munich, Winifred corresponded with Hitler, who was serving his prison sentence at the Landsberg fortress, and even sent packages to him. He received everything from her "that a supposed genius might need," including "large amounts of typewriter paper" and accessories which enabled him to begin writing *Mein Kampf*.[23] Once released after his short sentence, he came to Bayreuth regularly, giving the ailing Festspiele organization support, especially through financial means, but also through the presence of the entire National Socialist elite. They were indeed impressed, as the mention of Winifred in Goebbels' diary entry of May 8, 1926, made perfectly clear: "An attractive, fascinating woman. They should all be like that. And fanatically on our side." On December 19, 1928, she became one of the signers of the founding manifesto of the "Kampfbund für deutsche Kultur" (Militant League for German Culture).[24]Winifred's husband Siegfried died on August 4, 1930. The widow would gladly have begun a new relationship with Adolf Hitler. Four children may have resulted from her marriage with Siegfried, but in fact Siegfried did not take after his father

---

[22] Ernst Klee, *Das Personenlexikon zum Dritten Reich: War war was vor und nach 1945* (Frankfurt am Main, 2007).
[23] Bernd Mayer, *Bayreuth, die letzten 50 Jahre* (Bayreuth, 1988)
[24] Ibid.

very much in romantic matters. While it was known that Richard Wagner repeatedly demonstrated his healthy appetite for the ladies – there were, for example, Mathilde Wesendonck (1828-1902), Jessie Lanssot, the wife of a wealthy wine dealer from Bordeaux, with whom he even wanted to set out for Asia, and the little lady from Biebrich am Rhein – his son went in a different direction after fulfilling his marital duties. After his death, as a widow, Winifred's glowing eyes demonstrated her obvious interest in Adolf Hitler. Friedelind (1918-1991), her daughter, fittingly confirmed the rumors when she answered questions to this effect in her heavy Bayreuth Franconian dialect: *Mei Mudda mechat scho, oba da Hitler moch fei ned .... (My mother wants to, but Hitler obviously doesn't.)*

Women were in fact only of marginal interest to Adolf Hitler. As is well known, he only married his Eva Braun, unnecessarily, in the Führer's bunker in Berlin at the very end of his life.

After Siegfried, Winifred took over the management of the Bayreuth Festspiele, which she forged into a central Nazi cult site in the following years. The Intendant of the Berlin Staatsoper, Heinz Tietjen (1881-1967), served as the Artistic Director. Hitler was a regular guest at the Festspiele as of 1933. Beginning in 1936, he lived in the so-called Siegfried Wagner House, the wing built on to the left side of Haus Wahnfried. As of 1940, he no longer attended the Bayreuth Festspiele.[25]

---

[25] Ernst Klee, *Das Personenlexikon zum Dritten Reich: War war was vor und nach 1945* (Frankfurt am Main, 2007).

Until all German theaters were closed and the last Festspiele were held in 1944, Kriegsfestspiele (war festivals) were put on for purposes of propaganda, upon Hitler's orders. The audience consisted for the most part of wounded soldiers, their travel arrangements provided by the organization "Kraft durch Freude" (Strength through Joy). None of these changes succeeded in shaking Winifred's convictions. As late as October 16, 1944, she wrote in a public vow of loyalty to Hitler: "... [H]e has risen up into the heroic, is our Führer, through the night to the light."[26]

Alfred Ernst Rosenberg, born in the Baltic city of Reval on January 12, 1893, had lived through the revolution in Russia as a young man in 1917. Like the Russian rightists, he blamed it on a "Jewish-Masonic world conspiracy." By this time, he was already married, his wedding to Hilde Leesmann having taken place in 1915. His wife's family had close relationships with the better society in St. Petersburg, and he had enjoyed these contacts since his wedding.[27, 28]

Alfred Rosenberg was familiar with the works of Schopenhauer (1788-1860), Nietzsche (1844-1900) and, finally, Chamberlain's writings on Goethe and Kant.[29] Especially as of the beginning of his architecture studies in the fall of 1910 in Riga, he became equally interested in the antisemit-

[26] Ibid.
[27] Robert Wistrich and Hermann Weiss, *Wer war wer im Dritten Reich. Anhänger, Mitläufer, Gegner aus Politik, Wirtschaft, Militär, Kunst und Wissenschaft* (Munich, 1983).
[28] Ernst Piper, *Alfred Rosenberg, Hitler Chefideologe* (Munich, 2005).
[29] Walter Laqueure, *Deutschland und Russland* (Berlin, 1965).

ic writings and music dramas of Richard Wagner. He was enthusiastic about *Die Meistersinger* and *Tristan und Isolde*.

Following the Russian Revolution in 1917, Rosenberg (1893-1946) was transformed into a fanatic antisemite, came to Munich, and sought contact to similarly-minded circles.[30] Around 1918, he wrote his first antisemitic essays, such as "A Serious Question – The Jewish Question" and "The Jew." He used Wagner's modes of expression in these and advocated revoking the civil rights of the Jews.[31] Like Wagner, he claimed that there was a connection between "socialism, chaos of peoples and Jews." He postulated similarly that Jews were not capable of being creative artists and also claimed that they had no ability for state leadership.[32] Additional publications soon appeared in Munich: "Die Spur des Juden im Wandel der Zeiten" (The Jew's Trail through the Ages), "Das Verbrechen der Freimaurerei, Judentum, Jesuitismus, Deutsches Christentum" (The Crime of Freemasonry, Judaism, Jesuitism, German Christianity), and "Börse und Marxismus oder der Herr und der Knecht" (Stock Exchange and Marxism or the Master and the Servant). Worth mentioning, too, is the antisemitic essay "Der staatsfeindliche Zionismus" (Zionism, the Enemy of the State).

There is also a clear link to the statements of Richard and Cosima Wagner, and to those of Chamberlain, when Rosenberg writes: "Zionismus is … a way for ambitious speculators to develop a new staging area for their world

---

[30] Alfred Rosenberg, *Letzte Aufzeichnungen: Nürnberg 1945/46* (Uelzen, 1996).
[31] Ibid.
[32] Ibid.

usury."[33] Rosenberg's theory involved Jews whose single objective was that of undermining the existence of all other peoples. This "Jewish-Bolshevik impertinence" was one of the enemies against which Hitler and National Socialism as a whole needed to wage war.

In 1923, Rosenberg penned a commentary to the "Protocols of the Elders of Zion," which Hitler adopted and in part quoted in *Mein Kampf:* "Today, in the midst of the collapse of an entire world, a new epoch is beginning .... [O]ne of the signs of the coming struggle for a new world order is the recognition of the essence of the demon of our present decline."[34]

Also in 1923, Rosenberg became the editor-in-chief of the *Völkischer Beobachter.* He had already been its executive editor since 1921 and was its publisher as of 1938. He was one of the activists in the march on the Munich Feldherrnhalle, the so-called Beer Hall Putsch. While Hitler was serving his prison sentence in Landsberg am Lech following the failed coup attempt, he transferred the leadership of the now prohibited NSDAP to Alfred Rosenberg, who had not been convicted.[35]

What is arguably Rosenberg's most important antisemitic publication – *Der Mythos des 20. Jahrhunderts* (The Myth of the 20th Century) – was intended to be a continuation

---

Francis Nicosia, "Ein nützlicher Feind. Zionismus im nationalsozialistischen Deutschland 1933-1939," in *Vierteljahreshefte für Zeitgeschichte, Vol. 37, No. 3* (Munich, 1998).

[34] Alfred Rosenberg, "Die Protokolle der Weisen von Zion und die jüdische Weltpolitik," (München, 1933) cited from: Norman Cohn, *Das Ringen um das tausendjährige Reich* (Bern, 1961).

[35] Albrecht Tyrell, *Führer befiehl ... Selbstzeugnisse aus der Kampfzeit der NSDAP* (Bindlach, 1991).

of Chamberlain's *The Foundations of the 19th Century* and achieved a hardly imaginable total print run of almost two million copies. According to Rosenberg, Christianity needed to be cleansed of all Jewish influences (through the Old Testament). A new "metaphysics of race," an "Aryan race," was to be created, the only one that would be capable of cultural statements and achievements – particularly in the arts. In line with this approach, even Jesus, the founder of the religion, was stamped as an Aryan. To support this thesis, it was claimed that there were no Jews at all in the place he was born at that time.

Rosenberg constantly rendered homage to a powerful leader and thus helped to reinforce the National Socialist ideology. The master race, the Aryans, as a "pure race," should have the right to rise above the lower, "impure" race of the Jews. It is also for this reason that sexual relations between Aryans and Jews were punishable by death.

Rosenberg became a Reichsleiter in 1933. With his Reichsministerium for the Occupied Eastern Territories, he was then in a position to carry out the confiscation of Jewish property and valuable art treasures upon the direct order of the Führer as of 1941. These included the Amber Room in St. Petersburg, which is still missing today.[36]

In 1941, Rosenberg dedicated his *The Party Program: Essence, Principles and Goals of the NSDAP*, which had first been published in 1922, to Adolf Hitler. In the preface to this edition – which included copies number 101,000 to 150,000 – are striking catchwords:[37] "... [T]he awakening

---

36 Alfred Rosenberg, *Der Mythos des 20. Jahrhunderts* (Munich, 1988).
37 Alfred Rosenberg, Das Parteiprogramm. Wesen, Grundsätze und Ziele der NSDAP (Munich, 1941).

of the deep pride in the German people will begin with the victory over everything that is base, greedy. A new youth is maturing in the service of German values, and an iron will has been born which will avenge the offences of November 9, 1918, and will shake off the foreign yoke.... [N]ational Socialism regards this character development as a central problem of our times ...." Sentenced to death in Nuremberg in 1946, Alfred Rosenberg was executed there on October 16, 1946.

Joseph Goebbels, born in Rheyt on October 29, 1897, studied German and History from 1917 to 1921 at the Universities of Bonn, Freiburg, Würzburg, Munich and Heidelberg, and was awarded his doctorate by the Ruprecht Karls University in Heidelberg on April 21, 1922, with a dissertation entitled "Wilhelm von Schütz as a Dramatist."

Shortly after his doctorate was conferred, Else Janke, a teacher and the daughter of a Jewish mother and a Christian father, became his new girlfriend. Goebbels would have married her if she had not been a "half-breed." At the end of 1926, when he became the Gauleiter of Berlin, he ended the relationship with her.

In August 1924, he took part in the Founding Congress of the National Socialist Movement of Greater Germany in Weimar. In October 1924, he became the editor of its Elberfeld district propaganda publication, *Völkische Freiheit.* In 1925, when Hitler was released from prison in Landsburg and re-established the NSDAP, which had been banned in the interval, Goebbels became a member and, shortly thereafter, head of the Rhineland North Gau. On October 1st, Joseph Goebbels became the editor of the

National Socialist Letters, published by Gregor Strasser (1892-1934).[38]

Goebbels saw a direct connection between socialism and antisemitism and noted in 1925 that they were not all that different. Moreover, 100 slaveholders were tyrannizing all of Germany. And these slaveholders were the Jewish businessmen who had affiliated themselves with the bourgeois camp. Goebbels concluded that banning the Jews could not be the complete solution.[39]

Goebbels' views on the "Jewish question" varied from a terminable right of residence to an "eradication," "elimination" or "ruthless fight" against them: "Oh God, a communist, a rascal, a stateless so-and-so, a traitor, a swindler – a Jew! Beat him to death! That's it! Is it really that simple? The crux of the matter is the social question, how we, laborers and other citizens, can live together in the future."[40]

On November 9, 1926, Hitler named Goebbels as the Gauleiter of Berlin-Brandenburg. Demonstrations and battles in halls and on the street were followed by actions against Jews. During a screening of the American film "All Quiet on the Western Front," based on the novel by Erich Maria Remarque, in December 1930, Goebbels deployed brutal rowdies, who also attacked Jews. The film was finally dropped because it "endangered Germany's image," and Goebbels considered this a personal triumph.[41]

---

[38] Ralf G. Reuth, *Zettelkatalog BSB* (München, 1990).
[39] Claus Ekkehard Bärsch, *Der junge Goebbels, Erlösung und Vernichtung* (Munich: Verlag Wilhelm Fink, 2004).
[40] Ulrich Höver, *Joseph Goebbels, ein nationaler Sozialist* (Bonn, 1992).
[41] Ralf G. Reuth, *Zettelkatalog BSB* (München, 1990).

Goebbels now described the Jews as enemies of the people and parasites, and said that they would use their "right to hospitality" to cheat the German people and take advantage of them. So the Germans had no other choice but to defend themselves against the mania of gold. Goebbels took advantage of the latent general antisemitism and pointed out the destructive influence the Jews had, particularly in culture and art.

Here it is especially clear that, even in the terminology it used, the National Socialists simply assimilated what Wagner had already pre-formulated and thought. After all, for him the Jews were like "worms" that "putrefied" the body of the people. Goebbels used this "brown thread" and drew it out even further. Antisemitism thus became a cruel weapon – and not only as a means of propaganda – against the Jews.[42] On March 20, 1927, Jews in Berlin were beaten by Goebbels' SA men, and on September 12, 1931, hordes of young people battered passers-by who looked Jewish.[43]

Joseph Goebbels, who had been the Reichsminister for "Enlightenment and Propaganda" since March 13, 1933, now controlled the press, radio, film, theater, all printed materials, the visual arts, music, opera and concerts.[44] Film was Goebbels' particular favorite. As president of the Reichskulturkammer, he also used any possible opportunities to remove Jews from the cultural sector. For example, he expanded the Race Laws of 1935, created the terms

---

[42] Christian T. Barth, *Goebbels und die Juden* (Paderborn, 2003).
[43] Dirk Walter, *Antisemitische Kriminalität und Judenfeindschaft in der Weimarer Republik* (Bonn, 1999).
[44] Karl-Günter Zelle, *Joseph Goebbels: Aussen- und Innenansichten eines Propagandisten* (Berlin, 2010).

"half-Jew" and "quarter-Jew," and went about discriminating against people married to "half-Jews" or "quarter-Jews."

On June 16, 1936, however, he lamented to Fritz Sauckel (1894-1946): "What should one do in the arts? You can't simply fabricate artists. But this eternal waiting in the drought is awful, too. I'm going to get to work again now to weed out the bad ones." This means the Jews, of course. Goebbels now increased his efforts to isolate the Jews in Germany, and especially in Berlin, in all areas of life. In June 1938, more than 800 Jews had already been arrested. Jewish shops were marked as such, their windows smashed, and their merchandise plundered. Goebbels' implicit goal was for Berlin to be "judenrein" (cleansed of Jews). He shared Hitler's objective of having Germany free of Jews in ten years.[45] The first idea was to have them all deported to Madagascar.[46]

The cruel and excessive steps taken against the Jews during the so-called Reichspogromnacht (Night of Broken Glass) from November 9th to 10th, 1938 – the anniversary of the failed Hitler coup in Munich – took place at Goebbels' command. At a subsequent meeting of the party leadership, which was initially still critical of this approach, Goebbels demanded in an unambiguous speech that the party not interfere with anti-Jewish actions in the future: "I raise this matter with the Führer. He decides: Let the demonstrations continue. Call back the police. The Jews should feel the public scorn. This is only right. I immediately give the appropriate instructions to the police and the

---

[45] Christian T. Barth, *Goebbels und die Juden* (Paderborn, 2003).
[46] Toby Thacker, *Joseph Goebbels: Life and Death* (London and New York, 2009).

Party. Then I speak briefly to the Party leadership. ... [N]ow the people will act." Subsequently, thousands of synagogues and houses of worship in Germany were set on fire, Jewish shops were demolished, some 100 Jews were killed, and 30,000 were arrested.[47]

In Goebbels' presence, Hermann Göring (1893-1946) held a meeting with weighty consequences. A "fine" of a billion Reichsmarks was imposed on the German Jews as a whole, and insurance benefits that would be due to them were to be paid to the state. They were to be driven out of business life once and for all, to force them to emigrate. Their social exclusion was also to be increased. They were forbidden from attending "German" schools, movies and theaters, they were no longer permitted to own cars or motorcycles, and their protection as tenants in apartment houses was limited. Goebbels issued even more stringent measures for Berlin. Here Jews were also forbidden to visit swimming pools, the circus, or the zoo. Now actions were taken to remove Jewish tenants from "large apartments."[48]

To Goebbels it was absolutely essential for the Jews to be removed completely from Berlin and from Germany beginning in 1940. In 1941, he introduced the yellow badge bearing the Star of David, to make Jews even more clearly recognizable as persons to be defamed and excluded from German society. Their food rations were also reduced, and their homes were marked. The first deportations to the east began in October 1941, along with construction of the

---

[47] Christian T. Barth, *Goebbels und die Juden* (Paderborn, 2003).
[48] Ibid.

extermination camps. By March 1943, almost all Jews had been removed from Berlin.[49]

Goebbels may have no longer been directly involved in the decisive phase of the murder of the European Jews, and he might not have been informed about every detail. It is possible that it was only in 1942 that Goebbels actually learned the details regarding the annihilation of the Jews in the concentration camps, as can be seen in an entry in his diary, but their fate did not stir him: "The Jews are now being deported eastward from the Generalgouvernement, beginning with Lublin. A method is being used that is rather barbarian and cannot be described in detail here, and not much remains of the Jews themselves. ... [J]udgment is carried out on the Jews that is barbarian, but which is completely justified for them. The prophecy the Führer made for them, since they brought about a new world war, is beginning to come true in the most terrible of ways." And in April 1943 he stated: "I am convinced that by freeing Berlin from the Jews, I have accomplished one of my greatest political feats."[50]

On April 22, 1945, Goebbels moved to Hitler's Führer bunker in Berlin with his wife and children and was a witness on April 29th when Hitler and Eva Braun married late in their lives. Hitler appointed him Reichskanzler and then committed suicide on May 1, 1945. After killing his children, Goebbels and his wife also committed suicide. The

---

[49] Karl-Günter Zelle, *Hitlers zweifelnde Elite: Goebbels – Göring – Himmler – Speer* (Paderborn, 2010).
[50] Christian T. Barth, *Goebbels und die Juden* (Paderborn, 2003).

half-charred corpses were finally burned in 1970 and sunk in the Elbe.[51]

In view of these events, his grandiose pronouncement in 1936 seems especially spine-chilling for posterity: "For the arts, too, the people are the source of all our efforts. The artist must direct his work toward the people, as well. We have German theater, German film, German press, German literature, German visual arts, German music and German radio. The argument that has often been used against us, that it would not be possible to remove the Jews from artistic and cultural life, because there were too many of them and we would not be able to fill the empty spots, has been brilliantly refuted. This change in personnel, system and direction has been carried out without the least bit of friction or stagnation. And never before have German artists been so highly honored in Germany, or the arts so popular and respected."

Adolf Hitler was the dictator of the German Reich from 1933 to 1945. There are some 23 million Google entries under his name today, and it has long since ceased to be possible to list the written materials about him.

Hitler himself said that he went to the theater early in his life. He mentions performances in the Upper Austrian capital of Linz, which had a well-respected theater ensemble around 1900. At about twelve years of age, he saw *Wilhelm Tell* for the first time, as well as Richard Wagner's *Lohengrin* and *Rienzi*. Hitler later commented to his friend August Kubizek regarding the title role in the latter of these

---

[51] V.K. Vinogradov, J.F. Ponogyi and N.V. Tepzov, *Hitler's Death: Russia's last great secret from the files of the KGB* (London, 2005).

early Wagnerian works: "That's the moment it all began." And: "I wanted to become a tribune." In the years 1908 and 1909, as Kubizek related it, Hitler was more interested in Wagner's operas than in politics.[52] At first it wasn't *Lohengrin* that fascinated him but *Rienzi*, which most appealed to him and in which he felt his being was fully mirrored.

That the work had to do with a usurper, a dictator, who comes to power unlawfully and at the end is even murdered, did not disturb Hitler at all. Nor did the fact that Wagner later described this *Last of the Tribunes* as a folly of his youth. As the leader of the German Reich, Hitler had an opportunity to make Rienzi a victor. Was Hitler a victor?

Again and again, the "Führer" experienced great moments of this music drama. His enthusiasm for Richard Wagner was virtually boundless. But during his school days in Linz, he also delved into the ideology of the radical antisemite Georg von Schönerer (1842-1921).[53] In the fall of 1919, Hitler became acquainted with the antisemitic author Dietrich Eckart (1868-1923) and his writings. Eckart arranged contacts for him in the Munich bourgeoisie, as well as important sponsors. As of 1921, he introduced him there as the future charismatic far-right "Führer" and savior of the German nation.[54]

---

[52] Saul Friedländer and Jörn Rüsen, *Richard Wagner im Dritten Reich. Ein Schloss Elmau Symposium* (Munich, 2000).
[53] Brigitte Hamann, Hitlers Wien, *Lehrjahre eines Diktators* (Munich, 2012).
[54] Dietrich Eckart in Hermann Weiss, *Biografisches Lexikon zum Dritten Reich* (Frankfurt am Main, 1998).

In 1919, Adolf Hitler worked for the news and propaganda department of the Reichswehr, the German armed forces, in Munich. Presumably on September 16, 1919, he wrote a letter on behalf of his superior officer, Captain Karl Mayr. This antisemitic letter dealing with the necessity of destroying the Jews is addressed to Adolf Gemlich and, together with Hitler's political testament of April 29, 1945, serves as a disturbing manifestation of his thoughts: "If the Jew's feelings lie in the purely material, this is even more so in his way of thinking and striving. ... [H]is actions will result in a racial tuberculosis of the peoples. And this will occur: Antisemitism based on purely emotional grounds will find its ultimate expression in the form of pogroms. An antisemitism based on reason, however, must lead to a methodical, legal suppression and elimination of the privileges of the Jews, which only they possess in contrast to other aliens living among us (Aliens Law). The absolute ultimate objective, however, must be the complete and permanent removal of the Jews. Both of these can only be achieved by a government with national power, never by a government with national powerlessness."

In a keynote address on August 13, 1920, these views were presented in greater detail: Under the title "Why are we antisemites?" Hitler explained more clearly than ever before, due to their supposedly unalterable racial characters, why no Jews are able to perform constructive work. By their very nature, they are parasites and would do everything they can to attain world domination, by mixing the races, by misleading people through the arts and the press they control, by promoting class struggle, and even through prostitution.

Preventing this would be a central program point for National Socialism.[55]

Whereas Wagner merely spoke of a threat to the world from "dangerous Judaism," Hitler predicted as early as 1922 that which he and the National Socialists actually implemented in the most terrible way: "… [W]hen I have truly achieved power, the destruction of the Jews will be my first and most important task. As soon as I have the power to do so, for example, I will have a row of gallows erected on the Marienplatz in Munich. Then the Jews will be hung, one after the other, and they will hang there until they stink. They will hang as long as permitted by the laws of hygiene, and as soon as they are cut down, the next ones will be strung up, and this will continue until the last Jew in Munich has been finished off. The same thing will happen in other cities, until Germany has been cleansed of the very last Jew."

On the "German Days" – September 1 and 2, 1923 – in Nuremberg, Hitler, Ludendorff and their supporters united the free corps Bund Oberland and the Bund Reichskriegsflagge (Imperial War Flag Society) under Ernst Röhm and the SA to form the Deutscher Kampfbund (German Combat League). On September 25, Hitler assumed the political leadership of the Kampfbund.[56] Winifred Wagner was present on these "German Days" in Nuremberg; and Hitler already paid his first visit to the Villa Wahnfried on September 3, 1923. Following Hitler's so-

[55] R.H. Phelps, Dokumentation: *Hitlers "grundlegende" Rede über den Antisemitismus* (Stuttgart, 1968).
[56] Martin H. Geyer, *Verkehrte Welt: Revolution, Inflation und Moderne, München 1914-1924* (Göttingen, 1998).

called "March on the Feldherrnhalle" (Beer Hall Putsch), the "Bayreuth Circle" surrounding Cosima Wagner supported his claim to become the "Führer" of the nation.[57]

Adolf Hitler wrote the first part of *Mein Kampf* while he was in prison in Landsberg. According to his own statements, he did not intend it to be an autobiography or a substitute for the 25-point program.[58] Here he unfolded the racial antisemitism he had been articulating with increasing force since the summer of 1919, with the political objective of the "complete elimination of the Jews." The main idea was a supposed racial struggle that determined the history of humanity and in which the "right of the stronger" will prevail.[59]

He understood the "Aryan race" to be composed of white northern Europeans, and especially the Germans. They were the strongest race, destined for world domination. In his eyes, the Jews had been their mortal enemy throughout world history. They also strived for world domination, so that it would inevitably come to an apocalyptic final struggle with them.[60] Since they have no power or nation of their own, they seek to obtain these as a "parasite in the body of other peoples," by destroying other races. As their drive for domination and destruction is central to their

[57] Gottfried Wagner and Abraham J. Peck, *Unsere Stunde Null: Deutsche und Juden nach 1945: Familiengeschichte, Holocaust und Neubeginn. Historische Memoiren* (Vienna, 2006).

[58] Othmar Plöckinger, *Geschichte eines Buches: Adolf Hitler: "Mein Kampf": 1922-1945* (Berlin, 2006).

[59] Barbara Zehnpfennig, *Hitlers Mein Kampf: Eine Interpretation* (Hamburg and Munich, 2006).

[60] Hans-Ulrich Wehler, *Der Nationalsozialismus: Bewegung, Führerschaft, Verbrechen 1919-1945* (Munich, 2009).

race, the Aryans can only protect their own race by destroying the Jews.

A passing remark revealed the extent of Hitler's cynicism in his view of the German Jews: "If at the beginning of the war and during the war we had simply gassed twelve or fifteen thousand of these Hebrew racial corrupters, while hundreds of thousands of our very best German workers from all classes and professions have had to endure on the battlefield, then the millions of sacrifices on the front would not have been in vain. On the contrary: Doing away with twelve thousand scoundrels at the right time might have saved the lives of a million orderly Germans who were valuable for the future."

This certainly does not yet testify to a final plan for the physical destruction of all Jews, but it does bear witness to Hitler's increasing radicalization on the path toward the final genocide.[61] Many of the individual themes of Hitler's early speeches, such as the supposed nomadism of the Jews and an alleged inability in the realms of art, culture and nation-building, were also drawn from the many varied writings of German antisemites. These clearly included, in 1919-1920, ideas borrowed especially from the Munich National Socialist Friedrich Krohn. Also represented, for example, was the 1912 edition of Houston Stewart Chamberlain's *The Foundations of the 19th Century* – and Chamberlain was, as we have already seen, certainly the most powerful intellectual heir of Richard Wagner's antisemitism.

---

[61] Alexander Meschnig, *Der Wille zur Bewegung: Militärischer Traum und totalitäres Programm. Eine Mentalitätsgeschichte vom Ersten Weltkrieg zum Nationalsozialismus* (Bielefeld, 2008).

The NSCAP program, which postulated a nonconfessional "Positive Christianity" as opposed to the "Jewish-materialistic spirit" within the framework of the "feeling for ethics and morality of the Germanic race," was also a basis for Hitler's political antisemitism: "I believe that I am acting in the spirit of the almighty Creator: By resisting the Jews, I am fighting for the work of the Lord." He thus represented a radical "salvation antisemitism," which he repeatedly stressed as a core of his thoughts and rigorously adhered to until his suicide.[62]

The "Boycott of Jews" of April 1, 1933, was prepared personally by Adolf Hitler, although he did not publicly reveal that he was its deviser and organizer. He discussed the law that was adopted on April 7, 1933, to re-establish the permanent civil service (which would exclude "non-Aryan" civil servants), but decided on a more moderate version in view of the political situation.[63] For by 1933, Hitler already had a rigorous ghettoization of the Jews in mind, a physical exclusion. They had to be "removed from all professions, ... locked into a territory in which they can endure, ... while the German people can look on, the way one observes wild animals."[64]

But as soon as Hitler heard of the death of Embassy Secretary Ernst Eduard vom Rath (1909-1938), he immediately authorized Goebbels to use the assassination as a pretext for the Germany-wide November pogroms. As a result, hundreds of Jews were murdered, tens of thousands lost

---

[62] Saul Friedländer and Martin Pfeiffer, *Das Dritte Reich und die Juden: Die Jahre der Verfolgung 1933-1939. Die Jahre der Vernichtung 1939-1945* (Munich, 2007).

[63] Saul Friedländer, *Nachdenken über den Holocaust* (Munich, 2007).

[64] Hans-Ulrich Wehler, *Deutsche Gesellschaftsgeschichte, Vol. 4* (Munich, 2008).

their property and were interned in concentration camps, and thousands of synagogues and Jewish cemeteries were destroyed. At this point, Hitler delegated the ongoing "Jewish policy" to Hermann Göring, Heinrich Himmler (1900-1945) and Reinhard Heydrich (1904-1942). They used legal means to treat the Jews like criminals and had them pay the "Judenbusse" (Jewish fine) for the damage resulting from the November pogroms.[65]

In a speech at the Reichstag on January 30, 1939, Hitler declared unequivocally: "I would like to be a prophet again today: If the international finance Jewry in and outside Europe should succeed in plunging the nations into a world war once again, the result will not be the Bolshevization of the world and thus the victory of Jewry, but rather the annihilation of the Jewish race in Europe."[66] This idea is repeated in a speech on July 16, 1941, this time before high Nazi representatives, in the light of the Soviet Partisan War: "... [I]t gives us an opportunity to rot out that which opposes us."[67] He gave Heinrich Himmler appropriate orders, and he increased the quota of the task forces immediately from 3,000 to 33,000 men. Hitler had regular reports given to him about these events as of August 1, 1941. In the first five months of the war against the Soviet Union, the strike forces murdered approximately 500,000 Jews.[68]

---

[65] Hans-Jürgen Döschen, *"Reichskristallnacht." Die Novemberprogrome 1938* (Berlin, 2000).

[66] Max Domarus, *Hitler, Reden und Proklamationen 1932-1945. Kommentiert von einem deutschen Zeitgenossen. Vol. 4* (Frankfurt am Main, 2009).

[67] Saul Friedländer, *Nachdenken über den Holocaust* (Munich, 2007).

[68] Ian Kershaw, *Hitler, 1936-1945* (Stuttgart, 2000).

On August 19th, Hitler followed Goebbels' suggestion that, like the Polish Jews, the German Jews should now also be forced to wear the yellow badge with the Star of David. In September 1941, pressured by many Gauleiters, he allowed the deportation of German Jews to the east, which he had previously only wanted to permit following victory over the Soviet Union. In so doing, he reacted especially to Alfred Rosenberg's suggestion of retaliating for Stalin's deportation of the Volga Germans.[69]

On October 25, 1941, Hitler again repeated to his confidants his proclamation of January 30, 1939, that, in case of a new world war, the Jews were to be destroyed as retribution for the German war victims. "This race of criminals has two million lives on its conscience from the World War, now hundred thousands more. No one can say to me: We can't simply send them into the morass! ... It is good if the terror precedes us, that we are eradicating Jewry."[70] On December 12th, a day after war was declared on the USA, according to Goebbels' notes, Hitler confirmed to the Gauleiters and Reichsleiters invited to the Reichskanzlei: "The World War has started, and the destruction of Jewry must be the inevitable consequence." The Jews need to pay with their lives for the sacrifices of the German soldiers in the eastern campaign.[71]

On December 18, 1941, Himmler finally noted in his duty calendar that, as requested, Hitler had confirmed the pre-

---

[69] Michael Wildt, *Geschichte des Nationalsozialismus* (Göttingen, 2007).

[70] Saul Friedländer, *Das Dritte Reich und die Juden, Vol. 2: Die Jahre der Vernichtung 1939-1945* (Munich, 2006).

[71] Heino Heinisch, *Hitlers Geiseln: Hegemonialpläne und der Holocaust* (Leipzig and Berlin, 2005. In it: Die Tagebücher, Part 2, Vol. 2) Joseph Goebbels: Entry of December 13, 1941).

vious actions of the task forces and commanded: "Jewish question / To be exterminated as partisans."[72]

The macabre final point was on January 20, 1942. Adolf Hitler had authorized Göring's commission to Reinhard Heydrich for the "final solution to the Jewish question" and also arranged the meeting that was to seal the fate of millions of Jews. Reinhard Heydrich explained: "Eleven million European Jews are to be deported to the east. The goal is their 'natural reduction' through slave labor, as well as 'appropriate treatment' of the survivors. This is how he paraphrased the intention to eradicate the Jews in the code language of the Nazi regime.[73] For the 'evacuation' of the already overflowing Jewish ghettos to make room for the newly deported Jews, three extermination camps were put into operation in occupied Poland beginning in March 1942. This also marked the beginning of the murder of deported persons immediately after their arrival, and in gas chambers."[74]

Records of the "final solution to the Jewish question" were kept by Adolf Eichmann, who was responsible for the central organization of deportations, where the systematic murder of the European Jews was planned. Thus, ultimately, Richard Wagner's wish was also fulfilled, for the results of the Wannsee Conference are already the answer to the following statement made by Wagner in "Jewishness in

---

[72] Peter Witte, Michael Wildt and Martin Voigt, *Der Dienstkalender Heinrich Himmlers* (Konstanz, 1999).

[73] Raymond Reiter, *Hitlers Geheimpolitik* (Berlin and Munich, 2008).

[74] Hans Mommsen, "Der Wendepunkt zur 'Endlösung.' Die Eskalation der nationalsozialistischen Judenverfolgung" in Jürgen Matthäus and Klaus-Michael Mallmann, *Deutsche Juden Völkermord. Der Holocaust als Geschichte und Gegenwart* (Darmstadt, 2006).

Music": "... [T]he Jew rules, and he will rule as long as money remains, the power before which all our doings and dealings lose their force." Only the downfall of the Jews would free "German" art from Jewish capitalism and egoism. And Wagner also clearly stated at the time: "... I cannot judge whether it will be possible to put a stop to the deterioration of our culture by forcibly expelling the subversive foreign elements, because powers are necessary for this to occur whose availability I cannot judge." These powers against "the subversive power of the foreign element" – the Jews, of course – were delivered by Richard Wagner to Hitler and his co-conspirators, as plans for a "final solution to the Jewish question," as was ultimately realized at the Wannsee Conference.

In an entry in her diary, Cosima Wagner noted "that R. rejoiced in jest" when he heard about the anti-Jewish pogroms in Russia and voiced the wish that "all the Jews should burn during a performance of 'Nathan.' "[75] Wagner differentiated between non-Jews and Jews. He compared the latter, as already mentioned, with "worms," "rats," "mice," "warts" or "parasites."[76] In 1881, he wrote to King Ludwig II that "I consider the Jewish race to be the natural enemy of pure humanity and everything in it that is noble."

In an entry by Wagner in 1881, he supplies specific ideas to Hitler for his Nuremberg Reichstag speech of January 30, 1939. Wagner: "... [T]hat the human race consists of dissimilar races that cannot be reconciled, and that the no-

---

[75] Cosima Wagner, Martin Gregor-Martin and Dietrich Mack, *Tagebücher Vol. 4 (1881-1883)* (Munich, 1982).
[76] Matthias Küntzel, "Zum Richard-Wagner-Jahr 2013," *Die Welt am Sonntag, April 28, 2013.*

blest of them rules the non-noble ones, and that by mixing them they do not become alike, but only make themselves less noble." Hitler enacted the race laws "For the protection of German blood."[77]

Heinrich Himmler often spoke in letters and speeches to subordinates, such as in the Posen speeches in 1943, of the command given to him by Hitler to carry out the "final solution" and recorded special instructions from the Führer on this subject in his private notes. Hitler himself declared publicly a number of times, beginning in January 1942, that his "prophecy" of January 1939 would now be "fulfilled." Joseph Goebbels characterized him appropriately in a diary entry on March 27, 1942, as a "steadfast protagonist and spokesman for a radical solution" to the "Jewish question."[78] On October 7, 1942, Hitler had Odilo Globocnik report to him on the murder of Jews in four extermination camps. In March 1943, he received the Korherr report on the murder (circumscribed as "evacuation" and "special treatment") of two and a half (actually more than three) million Jews. The code language was also mandated by Hitler.

After the war, Nazi perpetrators like Rudolf Höss (1900-1947) and Adolf Eichmann (1906-1962) testified to the fact that Adolf Hitler had given orders in the summer or fall of 1941 to eliminate the Jews.[79] Raul Hilberg also emphasized in the *Neue Zürcher Zeitung* of December 2002 that Hitler had made antisemitism into his "government program, which led to the murder of the European

---

[77] Ibid.
[78] Ian Kershaw, *Wendepunkte: Schlüsselentscheidungen im Zweiten Weltkrieg* (Stuttgart, 2008).
[79] Saul Friedländer and Martin Pfeiffer, *Das Dritte Reich und die Juden: Die Jahre der Verfolgung 1933-1939.* (Munich, 2006).

| 71 |

Jews."[80] Ian Kershaw supports these opinions when he writes: "Without Hitler and the unique regime he headed, the creation of a program to implement the physical elimination of the European Jews would have been unthinkable."[81]

Karl Schlumprecht, Lord Mayor of the City of Bayreuth, had recognized the inextricable links between Wagner's and Hitler's antisemitism. In the program for the 1936 Festspiele, in addition to the power of the composer Richard Wagner, and beyond the message emanating from his art, he praised the fact that no one had more deeply felt this than the creator of the new Germany, Adolf Hitler. He emphasized that it was "… certainly to honor the debt of gratitude toward the master" that Hitler "… after seizing power, helped the Bayreuther Werk to get through the years of financial crisis." The fact that the Festspiele no longer needed assistance from the Reich was "… a gratifying sign of how quickly our nation had regained its self-confidence under Adolf Hitler's leadership." And he consciously emphasized: "For the first time, a man has thus come to power in Germany who has fully recognized the significance of Richard Wagner's message and thus the importance of the Bayreuth Festspiele for the German people. … In fact, Hitler believed that his nature was similar to that of Richard Wagner, saying: "I understand today why, in my youth, Wagner and his fate meant more to me than so many other great Germans. It was certainly the same need for an eternal struggle against hate, envy and misunderstanding."[82]

---

[80] Emil Neubauer, "Political Science 2015" in: *Neue Zürcher Zeitung,* Dec. 10, 2002.
[81] Ian Kershaw, *Hitler 1936-1945* (Munich, 2002).
[82] *Bayreuther Festspielführer* (Bayreuth, 1936).

Printed on Pages 115-116 of the 1936 program was a letter from Wagner to King Ludwig II: "I can only explain my august friend's well-disposed opinion of the Jews by the fact that these people never touch on his royal domain. They therefore remain a concept, whereas we experience them. The fact that I am able to interact with several of these people on a friendly, compassionate and sympathetic basis can only be explained by the fact that I believe that the Jewish race is born as the natural enemy of pure humanity and everything that is noble in it. It is certain that we Germans will be ruined by them, and perhaps I am the last German who would be able to uphold Judaism, which already controls everything, as an artistic person."[83]

Also in 1936, Friedrich W. Herzog recalled Richard Wagner's statements in connection with the founding of the German Empire in 1870-71: "With Germany's rebirth and renaissance, the ideal of my art stands and falls...." Herzog adds that only Hitler finally correctly understood this remark and would apply it. Then he mentioned Friedrich Nietzsche's statement: "For an event to be great, two things must concur: The great spirit of those who create it and that of those who experience it ..." It is for this very reason that it is Hitler's historical achievement to have recognized the significance of Bayreuth. The Führer also thus moved the personality of Richard Wagner into direct contemporary proximity, when he stated: "Wagner is more than a great artist. His personality and his work give a symbolic form to the longing for the ultimate oneness. If the united German people honors him today, it also hon-

---

[83] Dieter Borchmeyer, *Richard Wagners Antisemitismus* (Bundeszentrale für politische Bildung, May 14, 2013).

ors the master who has shown by his colossal example that true creativity can finally overcome seemingly insurmountable obstacles."[84]

Even shortly before his suicide, Hitler had thoughts like this. On April 29, 1945, he claimed: "Above all, I oblige the leadership of the nation and their followers to strict adherence to the race laws and to relentless resistance to the contaminator of all peoples in the world, international Jewry."[85]

Adolf Hitler described himself as having a character similar to that of Wagner. Are Wagner's antisemitic statements in his writings and – as an increasing number of authors, media and directorial concepts also claim today – in his music dramas identical with those of Hitler and his murderous accomplices? It cannot be denied: There is a "brown" thread that runs from Wagner's, though undoubtedly more from Cosima's, antisemitism to the exclusion of the Jews, their persecution, and their extermination in the Holocaust. One might be able to say that there was some Richard Wagner in Adolf Hitler, but can one truly claim that there was already a Hitler in Wagner?

What kind of conversations did Hitler have during his visits to "Haus Wahnfried" in Bayreuth, when the "eradication of the destructive element," the systematic elimination of the Jews, was his main topic? Did Richard Wagner's son, his daughter-in-law Winifred, or the grandchildren of the composer have anything to say against this? Who would seriously assert that they and the population of Bay-

---

[84] *Völkischer Beobachter*, July 11, 1936.
[85] *Hitlers politisches Testament. Die Bormann-Diktate vom Februar und April 1945* – http:www.eurobuch.com/buch/isbn/9783813551112.html.

reuth had not known or read anything about Hitler's anti-semitic rants, about Rosenberg's and Chamberlain's inflammatory, antisemitic writings, about the speeches of Propaganda Minister Goebbels, and not noticed the fact that, little by little, all of the Jewish artists were being eliminated from the Festspielhaus?

Part III

Regietheater – German director's theater in the 21st century

3.1. Explanation of *Regietheater*

In the modern *Regietheater* in Germany, the power is firmly in the hands of the stage directors. This concept is almost completely non-existent in the U.S. and the U.K., where the aim of the production of plays old and new is to communicate the work's original purpose. This makes it a playwright's theater. *Regietheater* – the German word for "director's theater" – refers to the modern practice, one that mainly developed after World War II, of allowing directors or producers freedom in the way a certain opera or play is staged or interpreted, so that any specific stage directions which may have been provided in the original score or script can be ignored, together with major elements of geographical location, chronological situation, casting and plot. This style of opera direction, currently prevalent in Europe, gives the director so much freedom that the original intentions of the composer and librettist are often changed to a far-reaching degree. *Regietheater* insinuates the belief that a director's interpretation of an opera is as important as what the composer and librettist intended, if not more so.

3.2. German *Regietheater* in the 21st century

"What in the world is wrong with German theater?" asked pianist and conductor András Schiff after having experienced it in the cultural capital of Berlin. In America, German stage productions are often referred to as "Eurotrash" – a genre in which stage directors have the power of absolutist rulers. "Where does this obsession with self-expression come from," asks Schiff, "this sense of self-importance, this lack of respect? Why is there so little humility and modesty? And why are stage directors so panic-stricken at the idea of boredom? ... Is our daily life so hectic that we no longer have any time? Or do we lose patience much too quickly?"

Of course, opera performances often last several hours – especially in the case of Wagner. But, Schiff says, since the respective stage director "thinks he has to assert himself – he doesn't understand music anyway, can barely read music (there are praiseworthy exceptions) – he is all the more uninhibited in the way he runs riot on the stage. He changes the plot, as well as where it is set." The result, he continues, is: "Music and the stage generate discrepancies and contradictions that unfortunately lead to the large number of dreadful productions that haunt the modern opera world."[1]

This renowned musician criticizes the set and staging concepts from the point of view of the audience. As an opera singer in Germany, engaged for productions of this kind, he would have no opportunity to express his displeasure.

---

[1] András Schiff, "Was zum Teufel ist mit dem deutschen Theater los?" *Neue Züricher Zeitung,* Oct. 27, 2014.

If he did, he might have very negative experiences that could even destroy the rest of his career. So this not only has to do with stage productions that are appalling for the audience and poorly crafted. It also has to do with singer slaves, who are contractually obligated to sing on stage, surrounded by swastikas and Nazis – or to try to find work abroad. Of course, they are only able to do so once they have made a name for themselves in Germany. This means that they are forced to appear in such horrendous staging concepts in sets containing swastikas and Nazis. The fact that German singers are often hired to sing heavy roles in the Wagner and Strauss repertoire makes the likelihood of this happening much greater for them.

Of considerable importance in these reflections is the term *Werktreue*. Under *Werktreue* – remaining faithful to the original – in plays and music theater, we understand the re-creation of a work that exists and is cohesive, and thus has already been created, in a manner that does not distort the original. In present-day production concepts, especially in Germany and primarily for plays and opera, this *Werktreue,* that shows respect for the work and its creator, is lacking to an increasing extent.

Bernd C. Sucher defended this practice when, in his speech on the occasion of the 350th anniversary of the Munich State Opera, he explained that opera houses are not museums, are not institutions for conservation, and should not have this character. Audiences will always pine for a *Werktreue* that never actually existed. This regret would constitute a *regressive utopia of reactionaries.*[2]

---

[2] Bernd C. Sucher, *Takt 2* (Bayerische Staatsoper, Munich, 2003).

Peter Wapnewski, on the other hand, rejects this *Werk-Untreue* – or lack of faithfulness to the original – as a presumptuous formula that asserts that future generations – today's stage directors – are better able to understand a work of art than its own creator understood it. This view is already the common property of the interpreting hermeneutics. The so-called Regietheater has thus repeatedly pushed itself forward and posed the question of whether the individual will of the stage director can finally reveal the potential of the piece that is slumbering there, or whether in fact, with his own perfection, he is disdainfully replacing the author's desires, using the latter only as a hull, and whether he should or may abuse it to demonstrate his own creative will.[3]

The appropriate images of a definite decadence in German theaters were already visible in the practice of the arts during the decline of the Roman Empire. Performances were steered in different directions by ancillary components, as can be clearly discerned today, and criticized by at least the majority of the audience. Those that were responsible at the time were not interested in *Werktreue* either, but gave an avid event audience the brutality they wanted to see. The mythical King Pentheus was torn into pieces by baccantes, and Hercules was actually burnt at the stake. An adultress who murdered with poison was to be raped by a donkey in public, but the clever animal refused to participate in this nonsense.

---

[3] Peter Wapnewsky, *Richard Wagner, Die Szene und ihr Meister* (München, 1978).

3.3. *Tannhäuser* and the Nazis

András Schiff's observation, as described above, is evident in Germany in the 21st century in the dictates of the modern Regietheater. Theodor Adorno undoubtedly gave an impetus to this in his 1962 diagnosis of what he saw as a permanent crisis in Germany. In the meanwhile, it is also being manifested as a crisis in the presentability of operas. "The logical result," – as Barbara Beyer wrote in 2005 in her preface to *Warum Oper?* – "was to depart, at the latest since 1968, from the outdated aesthetics of opera, seen as a disdained symbol of bourgeois cultural values, and to institute the so-called *Regietheater.*" To accomplish this, it was necessary to defy the sacrosanct claim to absolutism of the closed systems. Any right to absolute authority would have long since elapsed. Now targeted provocations were needed, intentional irritations of mental, visual and aural habits. In line with the times would be a rebellious and critical attitude toward opera as an institution, as well as an independent artistic attitude on the part of stage directors, who needed to again bring political explosiveness into the German musical theater through their work.[4] A number of statements by prominent opera directors in *Warum Oper?* were aligned with this point of view:

Albrecht Puhlmann (p. 10) "… [O]ne has to consciously express things so pointedly that one can clearly see that continuously new shocks and unexpected experiments will lead to the far-reaching alienation of an audience that is pleasure-oriented and needs to be built up. … [I]f one regards opera as an extraterritorial area, where one feels

---

[4] Barbara Beyer, *Warum Oper?* (Berlin, 2005).

comfortable and recognizes what one has seen years before, this would mean the end of opera."

Peter Konwitschny (p. 27): "I have something against this operatic pathos and also enjoy throwing something in the face of this conservative audience that is so dull. ... [A]nyone who makes use of the stage, just to produce beautiful, perfect tones for a great deal of money, is simply abusing society."

Jossi Wieler (p. 75): "The operational structure (of an opera house) gives the stage director complete freedom. He can demand anything, and the singer is contractually required to do whatever the stage director wants."

"My basic technique," says stage director Frank Castorf, "is shattering things." He has been the Artistic Director of the Berlin Volksbühne since 1992. As a stage director, he produced Richard Wagner's *Ring des Nibelungen* at the Bayreuth Festspiele in 2013. After the premiere, he was booed for a full fifteen minutes by a furious audience, and Castorf took notice of this by grinning.[5]

If we follow the logic of these thoughts and examine what has been happening on stage most recently from the perspective of "our past," the compelling conclusion is: Objectively speaking, opera directors have been trying for years to effect a necessary performance ban for Richard Wagner's antisemitic music dramas, for their directorial concepts and sets repeatedly point out the composer's hatred of the Jews and his link to the extermination mania of the Third Reich. Here are two such examples:

---

[5] Wolfgang Höbel, "Meine Grundtechnik ist Zerschlagen," *Der Spiegel,* July 21, 2014.

At the Bavarian State Opera in Munich, director David Alden and his set designer placed a heap of black coal on the slant of the stage for the production of *Tannhäuser*. This makes the Krupp Group and its involvement in National Socialism most conspicuous. In the background of the stage is a white wall, upon which G E R M A N I A N O S T R A is seen in large letters. Railroad tracks lead through a hole in this wall, so that the audience automatically thinks of Auschwitz. As the story progresses, letters fall out of the sign, until only the following letters are left: N S T A. This, of course, is supposed to represent the NSDAP, the National Socialist Party.

Wolfgang Mehring staged *Die Meistersinger von Nürnberg* at the Opera House in Nuremberg. At the end of the third act – on the Festwiese – he showed the Reichsparteitagsgelände, the Nazi Party Rally Grounds. Jewish prisoners in striped prison garb crawled around on the ground.

Any number of such examples could be mentioned at any time, and there are additional episodes to report. Since 1980, I have repeatedly performed in Japan. In 1988, for example, during the visit of the Munich State Opera, I sang the role of Hans Sachs in *Die Meistersinger von Nürnberg*. Having sung this role no fewer than 163 times, I then accepted an invitation in 2005 to stage the *Meistersinger* at the National Theatre in Tokyo myself.

It is presumably superfluous to mention that I know the piece inside out, so to speak, and that I am able to read orchestra scores. In this case, this is particularly relevant, because I personally own a copy of Wagner's handwritten *Meistersinger* score. My objective in this project could hardly be overlooked in view of the stage design. I had moved the set and the staging in this production totally to Wagner's era.

After the premiere, I returned to Germany. On behalf of a Japanese television station, which had sent a camera team back specifically for this purpose, I was asked why I had offered a false content of the opera in Tokyo. After all, to put it briefly, in the third act, on the Festwiese, I hadn't had any Nazis on the stage. I had not staged "our past" – that is, Wagner's and thus Hitler's antisemitism – and was apparently thus not contemporary in the eyes of this critic. But how should one actually imagine the protagonists in a contemporary staging of this type?

Jörg Hakendahl and Pedro de Castro described a performance like this at the Dusseldorf Opera: "The premiere of Wagner's *Tannhäuser* became a scandal surrounding a Nazi opera. Abhorrent scenes were described that shocked the audience. Naked performers in transparent cubes were 'gassed' there. In the first scene, the so-called Venusberg, a family was murdered by Nazis, including Tannhäuser. There was plenty of blood, with swastikas all over the place, and SS uniforms were also present. The director, Burkhard Kaminski, said that he wanted to thus address the subject of 'Richard Wagner's antisemitism.' "

About a dozen members of the audience on that first night in Dusseldorf required medical attention during the performance due to the extreme psychological and physical stress.[6] Wolfgang Höbel's commentary in *Der Spiegel* was rather laconic: "The Germans murdered six million Jews, but when you remind them of this nowadays, they need a

---

[6] Ibid.

doctor." Höbel also observed that when films, both those from Hollywood and German productions, show Nazi crimes, they were and are invariably accompanied by "sumptuous" Wagnerian music. Opera directors had dealt with the racial fanaticism of the composer and Adolf Hitler's own Wagnerian cult – and they were right to do so.[7]

Olaf Steinacker pondered about this performance in the *Westdeutsche Zeitung* and came to the conclusion that the Dusseldorf production could only have offended a few die-hard Wagner disciples who, convinced that they are all-knowing despite their actual ignorance, have the need to protect their hero Wagner from any and all hostilities. For this production was verily not a scandal, and it was by all means protected as is all art.[8] This does, however, present certain questions: Who actually thinks about the violated interpreters when they are required – "… because of our past" – to act in Nazi uniforms with swastika armbands or naked in transparent cubes, and even have to sing under such circumstances? And how does one actually sing, if one is to present Wagner's and Hitler's antisemitism?

The "very prominent" German artist Jonathan Meese was to stage Wagner's *Parsifal* in Bayreuth – and almost did so. Meese uses the Hitler salute wherever he can, explaining: "It's good for the body, frees the body." During his 165-minute provocation at the Mannheim Schillertage, as was reported in the press, he not only incessantly used the Hitler salute, but also oral sex with swastika aliens. After

[7] Wolfgang Höbel, "Tannhäuser-Skandal: Im Land der Täter und Sanitäter," *Der Spiegel,* May 10, 2013.
[8] Olaf Steinacker, "Der heftig kritisierte Tannhäuser wird abgesetzt," *Westdeutsche Zeitung, May 8, 2013.*

charges were brought against him, Meese was acquitted. The essence was that all of his actions were covered by artistic freedom.[9] *Die Welt* commented that Meese is one of the most important artists Germany has at the present time.[10]

"The more time that passes since the Third Reich, the more swastikas are flaunted on German stages," as *Focus* editor Michael Klonovsky observed quite some time ago.[11] On the other hand, Lion Edler, in his argument in *Junge Freiheit,* sees no problem in the fact that this is still so prevalent. Klonovsky's lament about the swastika in German opera performances would be justified, says Edler, and he also agrees that Adolf Hitler is on the cover of the news magazine *Der Spiegel* more frequently these days than on those of the propaganda papers in the Third Reich. Just the same, Lion Edler believes that the topic continues to be extremely important. To the contrary, the totalitarian spirit that is widely propagated today in politics and society is an argument for "coming to terms" with it comprehensively. The expression "Beware the beginnings" thus has its justification.[12] As seen by Lion Edler, a daily dose of Hitler functions as a kind of contraceptive against the new "beginnings."

It should be noted, however, that, if the members of the audience are provoked by seeing swastikas and the gassing of Jews on the stage, which will more likely insult and anger them, they will not necessarily leave the theater sensi-

---

[9] Jan Küveler, "Im Zeichen des Hakenkreuzes," *Die Welt,* August 8, 2012.
[10] Ibid.
[11] Michael Klonovsky, "Auch du mein Apollo? Sogar in dem attischen Gott schlummert ein Nazi," *Focus,* 42/2010.
[12] Lion Edler, "Die so genannte Bewältigung," *Junge Freiheit,* Nov. 17, 2010.

tized and shaken. In fact, for many of them this may even result in a fascination with such horrors or a dulling of their senses. Cultural edification, including a differentiation of their emotions, would be the basis for an altruistic image of humanity, and thus best suited as a contraceptive against new "beginnings."

Returning to our point of departure: Occurrences on German stages and especially in the works of Richard Wagner also and particularly deal with "... beware the beginnings." And today the practically inexhaustible possibilities of the modern director's theater seem to irresistibly lean toward revealing the antisemitism in Richard Wagner's music drama. Wagnerian singers have to deal with Hitler today – and more than ever before – because "Richard Wagner is in Adolf Hitler" and vice versa, as was "demonstrated" by numerous internationally renowned academics on the occasion of the composer's 200th birthday in 2013.

Nevertheless, the Jewish architect Peter Eisenmann feels that the Germans should finally relax a little. It's over! People shouldn't keep running around, saying: "You are bad, you are bad!" This doesn't help anyone.[13] Let us be honest and add: We Germans may – "... because of our past" – only start to relax a little when we have finally stopped presenting Wagner's and Hitler's heroes, as well as the music dramas of this composer, as being full of discrimination against the Jews. Or is there another solution?

In the past decades, with the help of many hundreds of millions of euros in state subventions, German theaters

---

13 Peter Eisenmann, "Peter Eisenmann über Juden, Deutsche und Schuld, im Gespräch mit Chris Melzer (Deutsche Presseagentur)," *Focus*, August 10, 2012.

have been challenged to demonstrate Wagner's and Hitler's antisemitism in this composer's music dramas, and they have done so with seemingly great success.

Part IV

Foundations of German law: Freedom of expression. The state educational mandate.

4.1. Freedom of expression

Freedom of expression is defined in Article 5 Section 3 of the German B+asic Law. It states: "Art and science, research and teaching shall be free." The logical question that follows is: To what or to whom does this freedom apply? Particularly the "what," but also the "whom," are the core issues of many discussions that go far beyond the narrow legal considerations.

In efforts to clarify the "what," one can establish a rough grid containing three currents. Used in attempts to define this can thereby be formal, open or material definitions of art.

Seen from the formal perspective, art is assumed to be involved if, strictly speaking, the requirements of a specific type of work or an art form (such as an opera or a novel) are fulfilled. The open definition sees the characteristic feature in a multifaceted statement, so that an ongoing interpretation and manifold meanings might be possible. The basis of a material definition is a free, creative design, in which the impressions or experiences of the artist are expressed through the medium of a certain idiom so that they can be directly observed.

Protected by the word "whom" are all persons who are involved in artistic work. Anyone who participates in the production or marketing of works of art can invoke this definition. Article 5 of the Basic Law guarantees freedom of expression. This protects theater producers, composers, stage directors, set designers, and costume designers, as well as authors, etc., in the areas in which they can freely create according to their own stylistic and aesthetic standards. Regulations regarding the style of productions on the stage, for example, or their content are therefore not permissible.

Freedom of expression does not guarantee the right to unlimited freedom, however. This is laid down in the statement regarding personal freedom in Article 2 Paragraph 1 of the Basic Law, which clarifies that no person has the right to simply act as he pleases. Freedom of action in which any person were permitted to act "as he pleases" would make additional laws superfluous. Barriers that can be considered limit the freedom of action provided by the basic rights while justifying restrictions by the state. Such barriers do not exist in the case of freedom of expression. They can, however, result from other fundamental rights (so-called conflicting fundamental rights).

When citing Section 130 of the German Criminal Code, for example, which deals with incitement to hatred, the question arises as to which fundamental law substantiates this section as an appropriate barrier. One might refer to human dignity, as set down in Article 1 Section 1 of the Basic Law. Pursuing this line of thought, freedom of expression as practiced cannot constitute an offense in line with Section 130 of the Criminal Code. Assuming it fulfills the judicial definition of "art," it would be sanctioned by

Section 130 of the Criminal Code, and this limitation of the freedom of expression would be warranted.

4.2. The state educational mandate

The Federal Republic of Germany sees itself as a "cultural nation." It has not been expressly mentioned in the Basic Law up to now, but it was indeed unanimously called for as early as 2007 by the Bundestag's Study Commission on "Culture in Germany." Several decisions by the Supreme Court and Article 35 of the Unification Treaty of 1990 also explicitly refer to Germany as a "cultural nation." Derived from this, too, is a cultural and educational mandate. It is for this reason that the public sector in Germany provides sums amounting to approximately eight billion euros every year to support art and culture nationally, in the individual states, and in the municipalities.

On average, for example, 84 percent of the needs of public theaters in Germany are subsidized, while only the remaining 16 percent must be independently financed.

But why does the government in Germany finance art and culture to this extent and not leave this to the market? The father of economic liberalism, Adam Smith, already stated in his work on *The Wealth of Nations*, first published in 1776, that, parallel to the "invisible hand" of the market, which regulates the economy, the government bears an important responsibility to establish and foster such public institutions and facilities. Although they are extremely beneficial for a large community, their very nature makes it impossible for them to yield returns that are high enough to cover the costs that accrue. Accordingly, one cannot expect them to assume this responsibility.[1] From the point of view of the government or society, these "public institutions and facilities" are of great benefit to society and for this very reason are supported with public funds, since they could not otherwise be sufficiently provided or demanded. In Germany, this includes ... art and culture.[2]

This educational mandate is explicitly defined in the Constitution of Bavaria, which states: "Education should not only impart knowledge and skills, but also heart and character, as well as respect for the dignity of man ... in the spirit of democracy ... and in the spirit of international understanding."

What are the reasons that art and culture are fostered as "merit goods" in Germany? The more or less official basis for the cultural mandate can be found in German Weimar Classicism, particularly in Schiller, and especially in his writings on the "Aesthetic Education of Man." In his programmatic lecture "The Theater Considered as a Moral Institution," published in 1802, Schiller writes: "The stage is, more than any other public institution, a school of practical wisdom, a guide to our daily lives, a key to the most secret approaches to the human soul."

By defining itself as a "cultural state," Germany differs significantly from other European nations. This is the second, the historical and political, basis for the cultural and educational mandate. Whereas France, for example, sees itself as

---

[1] Adam Smith and Laurence Winant Dickey, *Inquiry into the Nature and Causes of the Wealth of Nations* (Cambridge, 1993).
[2] Armin Klein, Bundeszentrale für politische Bildung, Dossier: Öffentliche Kulturbetriebe zwischen Bildungsauftrag und Besucherorientierung (May 5, 2010).

a "nation" or "république," and England as an "empire" or "commonwealth," art and culture were and remain the key elements of Germany's own social and especially political national identity. The fact that Germany developed so differently from England and France resulted from the questions faced in the 17th and 18th centuries, first, in regard to nationhood and, second, in regard to the political role of the bourgeois class of that era.

In England, the question of nationhood was settled relatively early, and the middle class won its place in the political process without bloodshed in the "Glorious Revolution" of 1688. In France, national unity had been determined at the latest in the 14th century, and the bourgeoisie had gained power in the revolution of 1789. In Germany, however, the situation was totally different. Until the 18th century, "Germany" was divided into a large number of small principalities, and the newly emerging German middle class was for the most part powerless in this system of mini-states. For this reason, national unity was realized in Germany especially through a shared language and culture. Theaters, but also universities and higher-level schools, were the preferred sites of the German middle class, which could be formed here, although it had no political effect for quite some time.

Financing of the arts and artists lay solely in the hands of secular and ecclesiastical patrons at the time. As of 1714, for example, composer Johann Sebastian Bach (1685-1750), was obligated to compose a new church cantata for Sunday services every four weeks. Better remunerated as the musical director of the Thomaskirche (St. Thomas Church) in Leipzig, he composed, among other things, the St. John Passion and the St. Matthew Passion, the Christmas Oratorio, and over 300 cantatas. After many lean years, Richard Wagner enjoyed generous subsidies from the Bavarian King Ludwig II that enabled him to have his music dramas performed. In particular, this involved *Die Meistersinger* in Munich, as well as the *Ring des Nibelungen* and *Parsifal* at the Bayreuth Festival.

It should be noted that the historical principalities – in which individual rulers financed their theaters, musical ensembles and orchestras, as well as the composers, in their courts – were the forerunners of the fact that in present-day Germany there are so many theaters in relatively small cities whose financing often stems from their locality – their city or Land.

It was primarily touring Italian and French theater troupes that performed in the many theaters belonging to the individual historical principalities, duchies, earldoms and kingdoms. These were private enterprises, with an impresario who managed their receipts. Often enough, if there were too few spectators, such entrepreneurs were insolvent and were not able to pay their artists' fees after the performance. This is the reason that, until about 30 years ago, the old tradition was still in force of paying guest artists their fee for the entire evening in cash during the intermission, just in case the impresario was bankrupt.

Present-day Germany is a federation of 16 Länder (states). Each Land has its own government and a minister of education and cultural affairs. These individuals are recruited on the basis of their membership in the ruling party. They are not artists, but might be dentists, Latin professors, or anything else. Are they knowledgeable enough to hire the directors and principal conductors of the opera houses?

Today all of the opera houses in the 16 Länder are dependent upon subsidies from government funds and are categorized as Stadttheater (municipal theaters), Landestheater (provincial or Land theaters) or Staatsopernhäuser (state opera houses). For this reason, they are also subsidized in different ways, by the commune or the Land.

Over and over again, a heated debate is conducted publicly and in the media regarding the high financial subsidies, especially for opera. Politicians and soccer fans ask with annoyance how much opera the country really needs. According to a survey by the Berlin parliament, only a narrow majority of 58 percent are in favor of the transfer of funds provided by taxpayers to the opera. These subsidies are in fact substantial, considering the fact that 186.10 euros had to be added in 2009 for each ticket for an evening at the Berlin Staatsoper. For the Komische Oper, the sum was 181.10 euros, for the Deutsche Oper 171.40 euros, and in the case of the Volkstheater in Rostock as much as 402 euros. On the basis of its educational mandate, the state orders immaterial merchandise (music theater) and pays for it even though, protected by freedom of expression as guaranteed by law, the producer may not deliver this merchandise or may deliver a product that has not even been ordered. Needed here are politicians who would fill general manager positions for the supplier, in the name of society. Therefore one can legitimately ask what role is played by state or municipal cultural policy makers in this connection.

Far too many cultural policy makers base their views on a radical interpretation of freedom of expression and the autonomy of artists and retreat behind the administration budgetary resources that are generally truly very limited and are constantly being curtailed even further. Is that really enough for responsible cultural policy?

Of course, it is clear that politicians should not interfere with artistic creativity. But they can and should establish a material framework that will make it possible for good art to be produced, and they can and should encourage public discourse in society – one that involves the audience – about everything that has to do with culture, and especially art, perhaps even inspired through their vision. Cultural policy of this kind does not impose its will, but does not shrink from the administration of budgetary titles either.

There is probably hardly a municipal budget in which there have not been cutbacks. Politicians involved in culture make things simple for themselves when they declare that (unfortunately?) the budgets for culture have also been affected. Anyone who sees cultural policy in this way has failed to fulfill his commission in two different ways: Lack of knowledge regarding the social role of the arts and ignorance in dealing with the principle of economic efficiency, which has been stressed to an irrational degree.

This inappropriate self-reduction by cultural politicians concedes to the practice of culture and art an equally inappropriate latitude in the practically arbitrary ways they deal with works of art, especially where artistic reproduction is required, that is, in the performing arts. One could say that both sides distance themselves to an extreme extent and leave a wide gap free in which cultural politicians, discursively and with remarks, also search for forms of balance between freedom on the part of the performers and respect for the work being performed.

In the USA, for example, it is private donors who enable productions at the Metropolitan Opera that do *not* provoke their audience, that do *not* insert political scandals in *Hänsel und Gretel,* and thus remain true to the works themselves.

Emperor Joseph II of Austria had already clearly articulated the cultural importance of theaters when he proclaimed that they were to contribute to the refinement of morality and taste of the nation. (This was later voiced in the form of the state educational mandate.) "And this is why," wrote Richard Wagner, "we determine that the opera theater is to be an institution of the arts that will contribute to the refinement of public taste through consistently good and correct productions of musical dramatic works."[3]

Theaters were and are at all times a mirror of society, institutions that shape and satisfy essential human needs. However, in many places – and particularly in Germany – they no longer impart the values that would help to shape an *improved* individual and thus peaceful coexistence in a society. In our day-to-day life, we are already experiencing an entropy of values to far too great an extent, a dangerous weakening in man's ability to aggressively use culture to combat abysses in one's own values as well as those of the outer world. Unfortunately, our cultural and educational institutions in Germany often fail to fulfill their so highly subsidized state mandate. They satisfy the superficial desires of the "fun society" and thereby deny intense human emotions of joy and sorrow. Deeply experienced emotions involve a differentiation of the senses, a deeper structuring

---

[3] Richard Wagner, "Das Wiener Hof-Operntheater," *Der Botschafter* (Vienna, 1863).

of feelings, that which Richard Wagner describes in *Parsifal* as "through compassion made wise," an altruistic image of humankind, which is thus capable of democracy. This deficit may also be an explanation for the increase in brutality, intolerance, xenophobia and antisemitism that has been witnessed recently in our society.

Part V

A legal complaint against
Deutsche Oper am Rhein in Dusseldorf

In the hope of having an actual impact on the staging practices described in this book, I decided in October 2014 to take real legal steps against those responsible for the especially onerous production of Tannhäuser in Dusseldorf. Below you will find the content of my complaint against Deutsche Oper am Rhein, the response of the Public Prosecutor, and various related commentaries, naturally all in their English translations. Unfortunately, these efforts did not have any positive results. Similar steps by the wider public would, of course, be more than welcome.

5.1. My complaint with request for prosecution

October 27, 2014

a g a i n s t

General Manager Prof. Christoph Meyer
and Stage Director Burkhard C. Kosminski

both at Heinrich-Heine-Allee 16a, 40213 Düsseldorf, Deutsche Oper am Rhein

f o r

Suspicion of an offense against § 86 StGB (Criminal Code) (Dissemination of propaganda material of unconstitutional organizations)
and § 86a StGB (Using symbols of unconstitutional organizations)
and § 130 StGB (Incitement to hatred)

and § 131 (1) No. 2 StGB (Depictions of violence) and all other legal grounds.

On May 4, 2013, the accused persons, Meyer as General Manager and Kosminski as Stage Director, working together in conscious and willful collusion, produced Richard Wagner's opera, *Tannhäuser*, in which various serious offenses were committed concurrently through its performance.

The emphasis was not placed on Richard Wagner's music or on the plot of *Tannhäuser*, but on the wearing of SS uniforms, on swastikas, on the gassing of Jewish citizens, and on the shooting of Jewish families, as well as on other abuses, rapes and shootings of people by performers who glorified violence and displayed Nazi symbols, swastikas, and SS uniforms, none of which was associated with the plot of the Wagner opera.

On May 30, 2013, *Spiegel-Online* reported that the Jewish Community in Dusseldorf and the Israeli ambassador to Germany, Yakov Hadas-Handelsman, had rejected the staging used in this performance, and that the Israeli ambassador had commented that "any use of Nazi symbols is uncalled for."

The DPA (German Press Agency) reported that the shooting of Jewish families and the gas chamber scenes were met with outrage, and that the Jewish Community welcomed the cancellation of the production, saying: "The danger exists that the suffering of the victims could be trivialized through the over-inflated use of Nazi symbols. One must be very sensitive here."

The facts were again described in a May 10, 2015, report in the newspaper *Die Welt*: "SS men, executions, gas chambers:

In its *Tannhäuser,* Deutsche Oper am Rhein in Dusseldorf paraded Nazi personnel," etc.

The Jewish Community also described the performance as "tasteless" in the May 6, 2013, edition of the magazine *Zeit-Online.*

And on May 13, 2013, *Spiegel-Online* reported that the swastika armband was worn "with pride."

Depictions such as opera performances (see § 11 (3) StGB) like those referred to here also constitute propaganda as defined by § 86 (2) StGB (Criminal Code). This performance of *Tannhäuser* is directed against the concept of international understanding (see Art. 9 (2) GG (German Basic Law), and this is expressed in the propaganda in the performance itself, since the state is depicted as an "Aryan racial community." The members of a particular ethnic or religious group, here the Jews, are shown as the mere object of arbitrary actions. This is inconsistent with a free and democratic basic order.

§ 86 (1) No. 4 StGB is explicitly violated since acts of former National Socialist organizations, the NSDAP, the SS or divisions thereof or affiliated associations and their symbols, uniforms and actions are presented in a brutal manner. The motives of the persons responsible for this and the disseminators' intended purpose are unimportant.

The over-inflated use of the uniforms of National Socialist groups and of swastikas can engender a certain habituation to the use of such symbols, so that the acts committed by the Nazis are also trivialized within the meaning of § 130 (3) StGB.

The Jewish Community sees a danger in the fact that the suffering of the victims is trivialized by this excessive use and thus made to appear harmless in terms of the objective facts.

In the performance of *Tannhäuser,* acts of violence against people are depicted, namely aggressive behavior that directly infringes upon or endangers people's physical integrity (Decision of the Federal Constitutional Court 87, 227). The representations that are portrayed, in which people are gassed and executed without reason, are – in themselves – cruel and inhuman. They express a dehumanizing and ruthless inclination, as people are murdered out of context and "just for fun." The "heroes" commit such acts of violence while claiming to do something great, impressive or heroic, or make these killings appear harmless as a common and acceptable form of behavior in human life, or at least as an irreprehensible way of expressing conflicts. In contrast to a war film which is intended to communicate pacifist tendencies, the present displays, in the entire context in which the individual depictions of violence are embedded, are the expression that is to be communicated. A detached or alienated description is not provided; rather, the focus is specifically on the shock effect of unquestioned brutality that is used as a creative medium within the plot. The cruelty of this display is at the forefront and has a brutalizing and savaging effect, especially on young people, since these bloodthirsty events occur without any context, merely in order to produce disgust and thrills. Human dignity is thereby violated, and this is determined solely according to objective standards. A verbal caveat or distancing on the part of the accused from that which is shown does not preclude this violation.

As a result, members of the audience not only became increasingly outraged, but some of them experienced physical symptoms which required medical assistance. To what extent public outrage precludes social acceptability should not be further considered here, but actions that cause bodily harm to uninvolved persons are never socially acceptable.

In regard to the question of freedom of expression versus criminal offenses, see the relevant literature and comments to Art. 5 (3) GG. Particularly in the area of political offenses, the limits on freedom of expression as a justification are difficult to define. This is not so in the present case, however, as the presentation of violence and inhuman actions is in the foreground, and there is no reflection of an "educational mandate." Respect for fellow human beings and nature is a central theme of the educational mandate, emanating from freedom of expression and the communication of culture. In the performing arts, like opera, one speaks less of "creating," but more of "staging." The person who puts on a work, that is, who "stages" it and thus "directs" the production, is the stage director. This person must adhere to the educational mandate and the communication of culture. Even the representation of a "happening," containing the Hitler salute, swastikas, and extermination of the Jews, must be judged in terms of the communication of culture.

Therefore, there is a strong initial suspicion against the accused persons, and we hereby request confirmation of receipt of the present complaint as well as the complainant's request for prosecution, along with a file number.

Receipt of the criminal complaint has now been confirmed by Public Prosecutor B. File No.: 80 Js 1093/14.

5.2. The Public Prosecutor's response

Dusseldorf, November 24, 2014

Dear Mr. R.:

Under § 152 (2) of the Code of Criminal Procedure, the initiation of investigative proceedings against Prof. Christoph Meyer and Mr. Burkhard Kosminski as requested by your client (Bernd Weikl) requires the existence of sufficient factual evidence of an actionable criminal offense. This evidence must relate to the objective and subjective elements of an offense under the penal code.

The opera Tannhäuser by Richard Wagner, as produced in Dusseldorf on May 4, 2013, falls within the scope of freedom of expression, which is protected by the Basic Law (Art. 5 (3) GG). The criminal offenses being considered must be viewed in the light of this constitutional law and are subject to the limitation of social acceptability, which is explicitly governed by § 86 (3) StGB and is to be applied in accordance with the references in § 86a (3), 130 (6) and 130a (3) StGB. Furthermore, Art. 5 (3) GG is directly applicable. According to that provision, the relevant criminal offense is excluded if the act is committed in the service of art, science, research or teaching, to report on current events or history, or for similar purposes, as in the case at hand.

The opera is a classic form of art that falls under the area protected by Art. 5 (3) GG, along with all forms of art. It lies in the power of the stage director to interpret the work and to stage it. This interpretation cannot be assessed under criminal law. The stage director – together with the general manager, who shares responsibility – is also permitted to use shocking and drastic means without facing criminal charges. Art cannot be subjected to state control of its style or standards. The offensiveness of a performance does not eliminate its character as a work of art (see German Federal Constitutional Court [BVerfG], decision of March 7, 1990, 1 BvR 266/86, 1 BvR 913187, cited to juris).

Therefore, opening an investigation is out of the question.

Respectfully yours,

Public Prosecutor Ms. B.

5.3. My view and response to Dusseldorf

The arguments presented by the Public Prosecutor, as stated above, show that she is not familiar with the StPO (Code of Criminal Procedure). Under § 152 (2) StPO, the Public Prosecutor's monopoly over the decision to take a complaint to court results in an obligation to initiate an investigation (§ 160 StPO).

If she wishes to suspend proceedings due to a lack of factual evidence, this decision must be made in accordance with § 170 (2) StPO, and a notification with information on legal remedies must be provided to the complainant in accordance with § 171 StPO (Directive No. 89).

This complaint does not have to do with making "art subject to … state control of its style or standards," but rather with "depictions of violence" and "bodily harm," *inter alia.* It is true that portrayals of violence can be recognized as "art" and an expression of artistic freedom. They are protected under Art. 5 (3) GG (German Basic Law), which states:

"Every person shall have the right freely to express and disseminate his opinions in speech, writing and pictures, and to inform himself without hindrance from generally accessible sources. Freedom of the press and freedom of reporting by means of broadcasts and films shall be guaranteed. There shall be no censorship."

"These rights shall find their limits in the provisions of general laws, in provisions for the protection of young people, and in the right to personal honor."

"Arts and sciences, research and teaching shall be free. The freedom of teaching shall not release any person from allegiance to the Basic Law."

And what would happen if the image of Mohammed were to be shown in a drama or if he were to stand on stage and incite terrorism or be seen as a caricature?

Continuing with the Public Prosecutor's statements: "… [I]f the act is committed in the service of art, science, research or teaching, to report on current events or history, or for similar purposes…"

Who can truly claim that this entire unspeakable story, the demonstrated gassing of Jews in Dusseldorf, serves art (or anything else)? Certainly not the audience (which clearly booed at the end of the premiere), not the opera house (neither artistically nor financially), and thus none of the employees of the opera house. On what basis and in what way can Ms. B claim that this disaster served art? In fact, it

only served to benefit the bank accounts of the stage director and the set designer. This, however, is not a cultural as-
set that is worthy of protection.

5.4. Reactions from the audience

Mr. B. thinks that one ought to take a look at the libretto
of *Tannhäuser*. There, he says, one could discover unspeakable, bigoted and very Germanic kitsch. One of the
expressions often used in this work is "Heil," and the
Landgrave is also named Hermann – as in Hermann Göring. Is there any other way to stage this today? And then
there is Wagner himself – this "unfortunately gifted fiend"
– who lays mines in many of his works, full of antisemitism, chauvinism, and an odd view of religion! His descendants – Cosima, Siegfried, Winifred, Wieland and Wolfgang – would have indubitably "linked" his problematic
views to those of Hitler. Wagner's music and, in particular,
the still "romantic" *Tannhäuser*, became the "soundtrack"
of the Third Reich. For example, it is the fanfares from
Act II of *Tannhäuser* that are so familiar to us from the
Nazi propaganda films. So why shouldn't *Tannhäuser*,
above all, not be staged in such a critical manner?

Then Mr. W. brings up the matter of freedom of expression. If the Wagner enthusiasts and routine operagoers
find it too radical and sacrilegious, they could simply close
their eyes during the performance and listen to the music.
For a Mr. B., it was an exceedingly successful performance,
and he thanks the stage director for it.

Art that is not polarizing and that does not stimulate new
ways of thinking, suggests Mr. T., is not art. He goes on:

"This should be borne in mind by everyone who, without giving it further consideration, comments on a courageous, artistic effort in a way that shows so little real thought. What do they really think art ought to be like? One doesn't need to be an artist if one is to simply imitate approaches that are already familiar! This can also be done by imitators, parrot fashion. Even if you yourself don't like this, people, make sure that you do not fall into the trap of calling this 'degenerate' art or the like, just because it is inconsistent with what you yourself are accustomed to seeing. Each person must examine his own motives."

5.5. The Dusseldorf Jewish Community

The reactions of Michael Szentei-Heise, who heads the Dusseldorf Jewish Community, were provided in "Jüdische Gemeinde nimmt Wagner in Schutz" (Jewish community defends Wagner) in *Zeit-Online* on May 6, 2013. Szentei-Heise says that he believes that Wagner was an "ardent antisemite," but does not consider it "legitimate to retaliate on stage this way against the composer." Wagner's basic political orientation is not reflected in his music or in the libretto. "Wagner had nothing to do with the Holocaust," said Szentei-Heise, and the Dusseldorf production has "done an injustice" to the composer. Just the same, as Szentei-Heise continues, "It feels strange to have to defend Wagner."

5.6. The Chief Public Prosecutor in Dusseldorf

Dusseldorf, February 17, 2015

"Having considered the merits, I find no grounds to have an investigation opened. The decision of the Public Prosecutor is in compliance with the factually and legally relevant position in all respects." The German Chief Public Prosecutor remarks in addition: "According to § 152 (2) StPO (Code of Criminal Procedure), the Office of the Public Prosecutor may only conduct an investigation if it has sufficient factual evidence of a criminal offense. If – as here – this is not the case on legal grounds, the investigative bodies are prohibited by law from conducting any investigations.

"Since the client (Bernd Weikl) is not an aggrieved person within the meaning of §§ 171 (2) and 172 (1) StPO, the Office of the Public Prosecutor has also appropriately refrained from attaching a notification of legal rights to the contested decision. I therefore dismiss the appeal as unfounded in its entirety."

Part VI

Richard Wagner's music dramas: A promising concept for today's Germany

6.1. Introduction

In 1869, when Wagner distributed the new edition of his essay "Jewishness in Music," which had appeared anonymously in 1850, this triggered 170 published protests and attacks. In several cities, performances of *Die Meistersinger* were met with booing because of their antisemitic innuendos. Matthias Künztel names a number of renowned Wagner researchers whose studies come to the same conclusion, having found sufficient proof for the composer's antisemitism in his music dramas. Among the authors he mentions are: Marc A. Weiner, Paul Lawrence Rose, Barry Millington, Saul Friedländer, Hartmut Zelinsky, Ulrich Drüner, Annette Hein, Gottfried Wagner and Jens Malte Fischer.[1]

Modern stage directors and set designers willingly adopt this view. The production of *Tannhäuser* at the Deutsche Oper am Rhein can be considered an example they would find worthy of emulation. Since jurisprudence also guarantees the extreme application of freedom of expression in Germany, the shocking theoretical and radical staging concepts that follow would be very much in line with the spirit

---

[1] Matthias Küntzel, "Arien für Arier? Einspruch gegen den Wagner-Kult", *Die Welt am Sonntag*, April 28, 2013

of the times. The exaggerations that are contained demonstrate the serious danger of the trend that has been developing on German stages.

To clearly demonstrate the antisemitic explosiveness of the type of production concepts for works by Richard Wagner discussed in this book, detailed suggestions have been developed for these works that relate their content to the Nazi era. Concrete references to antisemitism, as claimed by various authors, and to the ideology of the National Socialists will be indicated briefly in brackets. The sets and costumes – Aryans identified by swastikas and Jews by the yellow badge with the Star of David – can also clearly identify the social positions of the various characters.

6.2. *Der Fliegende Holländer*
The Flying Dutchman

Since the 13th century, a story has been related that an unnamed contemporary of Jesus taunted him on what is now known as the "Via Dolorosa" and refused to carry the cross with him. Christ therefore cursed this unknown person, causing him to wander thenceforth and until the Second Coming and the Last Judgment, which would subsequently take place. In Leiden, today the third largest city in Holland, an anonymous document was printed in 1602 that referred to this unnamed mocker of Jesus. The author or publisher gave him the name Ahasuerus. This unknown person, damned for time eternal and ceaselessly wandering since then, has appeared as a Jew in various folk tales. In Spain, for example, he became Juan "Espera en Dios" (Hope in God) and ultimately, up to the present day, came to represent the hope that the Messiah would return, and not only among orthodox Jews.

Theologian and orientalist Johann Jacob Schudt (1664-1722) defined Ahasuerus in his Jüdische Merckwürdigkeiten (Jewish Peculiarities), published between 1714 and 1717, very much in line with Richard Wagner's statements and those of National Socialist sources: "This wandering Jew is not a single person, but the entire Jewish people subsequent to the crucifixion of Christ, scattered throughout the world, wandering, according to Christ's testimony, until the Day of Judgment."[2]

There has been much discussion about the emancipation of the Jews since then. Bruno Bauer, for example, wrote an essay in 1843 entitled "The Jewish Question." At almost the same time, in 1844, Constantin Frantz published the essay "Ahasuerus or the Jewish Question." It said: "The Jewish people itself is the Eternal Jew. It rejected the Savior, and therefore is scattered all over the earth and cannot find peace anywhere. It wants to mix with the peoples and thus destroy its ethnicity, and cannot do this."[3]

Divine punishment is now transferred from the individual crime committed by Ahasuerus to all of Jewry – as in the figure of the Flying Dutchman. Without a homeland until he is redeemed by an "Aryan blond" Senta, this finally leads to his death.

Richard Wagner must have been familiar with Constantin Franz's essay, and the writings and oral lore regarding the "Wandering Jew" would also have been available to him. In his "Mitteilung an meine Freunde" (Communication to My Friends) of 1851 – shortly after the anonymous publication of the anti-semitic pamphlet "Das Judentum in der Musik" (Jewishness in Music) – he calls the figure of the Flying Dutchman "an odd mixture of the character of the Eternal Jew with that of Odysseus." In this romantic opera, with his representation of the title role and thus his criticism of the Judaism he found so abhorrent, Wagner provided a template for the murderous ideology of the Third Reich.

National Socialism adopted it and used the figure for its antisemitic propaganda. In a speech to the SS leadership in 1935, Heinrich Himmler described the Eternal Jew as the "leader of the murderous subhumans." The hate the National Socialists had for the Jews was later made even clearer in the 1940 propaganda film "Der ewige Jude" (The Eternal Jew).

The legend of Ahasuerus is still used today for anti-Jewish statements. The "Engelwerk" of founder Gabriele Bitterlich (1896-1978) mentions in its programmatic handbook the "fallen archangel" and the "ghost of the accursed Jewish people." [4]

---

[2] Alex Bein, *Die Judenfrage: Biographie eines Weltproblems* (Stuttgart, 1980).
[3] Ibid.
[4] Heiner Boberski, *Das Engelwerk. Theorie und Praxis des Opus Angelorum* (Salzburg, 1993).

Characters:

- Daland, Captain of a destroyer during the Nazi era
- Senta, his blond, Aryan daughter
- Erik, a young officer in a fighter squadron
- Mary, Senta's older friend
- Daland's steersman
- The Dutchman, a wandering Jew, owner of an expensive sailing yacht

Place and time: Open sea, rocky coast, about 1940, and Daland's naval base, where the sailors' family members live

The Flying Dutchman

ACT I

Richard Wagner's description of the scene: "Steep, rocky shore. The sea takes up most of the stage. Cliffs in the foreground. Gorges on both sides, which produce echoes. Gloomy weather, violent storm." Daland's ship has dropped anchor. His crew is busy lashing down the ammunition boxes and are making a great deal of noise doing so. Daland goes on land. His sailors are singing, and their song is echoed by the cliff walls. The captain is unhappy about sudden complications due to the weather, but calms himself by ascertaining that the ground under the ship is safe. The island is named Sandwike, and wind is blowing out of the devil's hole. He says: "He who banks upon the wind banks on Satan's pity!" and goes back to his deck.

The Steersman is supposed to keep watch, but falls asleep. The expensive yacht with the blood red sails that belongs to the Jew Holländer suddenly appears out of nowhere and anchors not far from Daland's destroyer. The Dutchman, wearing black clothing, goes on land. In the monologue that follows, he laments his fate as a wandering, restless Jew. "The time is up, and once again seven years have gone by! Full of weariness, the sea throws me onto the land. Ah, proud ocean! In a short time, you will carry me again! Your defiance can yield, but my torment is eternal! The salvation I seek on land, never shall I find it! I will remain true to you, tides of the world's oceans, until your last wave breaks and your last waters run dry. How often have I thrown myself, full of longing, into the sea's deepest maw? But alas! I did not find death. There, in the awful tomb of ships, I drove my ship onto the rocks. But alas! My tomb would not be closed! Mockingly, I challenged the pirate, hoping for death in fierce combat. "Here," I cried,

"Show your prowess! My ship is filled with treasure." But alas! The sea's barbarous son crossed himself in fear, and fled. Nowhere a grave! Never death! This is damnation's dreadful command. I ask you, blessed angel of God, who won the terms of my salvation for me: Was I the unfortunate plaything of your scorn, when you showed me the way to salvation! Vain hope! Terrible, empty illusion! Eternal faithfulness no longer exists on earth! Only one single hope shall remain for me, only one shall stand unshaken. As long as the earth puts out new shoots, it must yet perish. Day of Judgment! Day of doom! When will you dawn in my night? When will it resound, the blow of annihilation that rends the earth asunder? [The Holocaust] When all the dead rise up again, I will fade into nothingness. You worlds, stop moving! Eternal destruction, take me in!" The Dutchman's crew [All Jews] repeat the last sentence.

Daland comes out of his cabin. His Steersman – assigned to keep guard – had fallen asleep. He is now awake and tries to make contact with the sailing yacht. The Dutchman answers and explains his situation: "I come from far away. Would you deny me anchorage in this storm?" "Who are you?" Daland asks him. The Captain of the large sailing ship: "A Dutchman." Daland: "Do you have any damage?" The Dutchman: "My ship is strong. She hasn't suffered any damage. Driven by storm and violent wind, I rove the seas. How long? I can scarcely say. I can no longer count the years. I think it impossible for me to name all the countries where I have been. But only one. The one I long for I cannot find: my homeland. [The wandering Jew] Grant me a short stay in your house, and you will not regret your generosity. My ship is richly laden with treasures from every region and zone. If you agree, it will surely be to your advantage."

Daland now asks the Dutchman what his ship contains, and the owner of the high seas sailing ship promises him the rarest of treasures: "Precious pearls, the noblest of gems. [The Jew doesn't work, but trades and lets others work for him.] Take a look and convince yourself of the value of the price I offer to you for friendly shelter, for lodging for a single night! What you see is only a fraction of what is stowed in my ship's hold. What use is the treasure to me? I have neither wife nor child, and I will never find my native land. I offer you all my riches, if you give me a new home among your people. If you have a daughter, let her be my wife! Fate has pursued me relentlessly; torment was my only companion. I shall never reach my homeland. If you will consent to this union, oh, then take my treasure." [It is a Jewish merchant who bargains. Strangely, Daland also demonstrates Jewish characteristics through his great interest in money and valuables.]

Daland has a beautiful daughter and agrees immediately: "I've wanted a son-in-law like this. You shall see her [The daughter], and if she pleases you…" The Dutchman interrupts: "She shall be mine. Will she be my angel? If, in the terrible violence of my torment, my longing for grace drives me on, may I cling to the one hope left to me? May I cherish the illusion that an angel may pity me? Then I would have reached the goal I had longed for. Ah, without hope, as I am, I still harbor hope." [He hopes for deliverance from Judaism.]

The two ships leave the anchorage ground and head for the naval base, thus also for Daland's daughter Senta.

ACT II

Inside a kind of crew's common room (recreation room or mess). Hanging on the wall is a painted portrait of a pale man wearing black Spanish attire. [See description of Spanish Jews as "Espera en Dios" (Hope in God or Waiting for the Messiah.]

The opera audience recognizes him immediately as the Dutchman from the first act. Senta is standing in front of the picture, looking at it as if in a trance. Mary asks whether she intends to spend her entire young life staring at this portrait. Senta answers by asking whether Mary herself hadn't spoken of the pale man in the picture.

Senta and Mary are not alone. The wives and fiancés of Daland's sailors are busy in the room, spinning wool. They are making warm clothing for the combat troops. This chorus of women and girls makes fun of Senta because of the picture and the way she keeps staring at this pale man. She is in love with a picture, they say, and they hope this will not cause a problem with the hot-blooded hunter Erik, who is really in love with her.

They ask Mary to tell the story of the Flying Dutchman. Mary doesn't want to do this, so Senta sings the ballad. "Have you encountered the ship at sea with blood-red sails and a black mast? On the bridge, the pale man, the master of the ship, keeps endless watch, without rest, without repose. Yet the pale man could find redemption one day, if he found a wife on earth who would be faithful to him until death! Ah! When will you find her, pale seaman? Pray to Heaven that a woman will soon be faithful to him. He once wanted to sail around a cape; he cursed and swore in mad fury 'In all eternity, I'll never give up.' Thus damned, he now roams the sea without rest, without repose! Yet, so that the poor man might still find redemption on earth, God's angel showed him the path to salvation! Ah! When will you find it, pale seaman? Pray to Heaven that a woman will soon be faithful to him! At anchor every seven years, he goes ashore to woo a woman. He has wooed every seven years, but never found a faithful woman. I am the one who will save you with my faithfulness! May God's angel reveal me to you! You shall find redemption through me!"

Mary and the other women are obviously shocked. They think Senta is mentally disturbed. Erik appears and announces Daland's return. Everyone rushes outside. Only Senta and Erik remain in the room. The young officer of the fighter squadron now becomes insistent with Senta, reminding her of the fact that her father would like to have a son-in-law. Admittedly, it should be a wealthy one. He is only an officer in the fighter squadron and therefore not rich, but does she – Senta – still care for him, and won't she convince her father? Senta interrupts him and wants to go out to her father, but Erik holds her back: "You are trying to avoid me. You don't want to answer my question." Senta: "You doubt whether I care for you?" Erik: "Your father, oh, he thinks only of wealth. Why do you keep looking at that picture?" Senta asks Erik whether it is forbidden to be inspired by a picture. But Erik had also heard her singing about her wish to be united with the Dutchman and that she would be faithful to him until death. Erik is suffering and lets Senta see this. "How great can your suffering be," asks Senta, "compared with the fate of that unfortunate man? Pity pierces my heart." Erik has already learned of this in a bad dream: "God protect you. Satan has ensnared you." [For Wagner and Hitler, the Jewish demon] In Erik's dream, Daland went on land with the stranger and Senta "kissed him with burning desire." Then the two of them "took flight onto the sea."

Senta, very agitated: "He is looking for me. I must see him. I must perish with him!" [The noble race is willing to make sacrifices, while the Dutchman thinks and acts egoistically, Jewish.] Erik, hopelessly and full of grief: "My dream spoke the truth!" He leaves.

Senta, toward the picture: "Ah, may you find her, pale seaman! Pray to Heaven that a woman will soon be faithful to him!" The father enters suddenly, and with him the Dutchman. Senta: "God be with you. Who is this stranger?" The father explains: "He is a seaman, long homeless, always on long voyages to distant places." And he is rich! "Banished from his native land. Tell me, Senta, would you mind if this stranger lodged with us?" And to the Dutchman: "Tell me, do you like her?" Turning to Senta again, he says she should be especially nice to him, for he has great wealth. Therefore the father wants to arrange his daughter's marriage right away: "He shall be your bridegroom." He shows her the many jewels the Dutchman has with him, then, not wanting to disturb the couple, he leaves the two of them alone.

This is followed by a long musical interlude, while Senta and the Dutchman stand facing one another, speechless. He finally begins with his declaration: "As from the distance of times long past, this maiden's image speaks to me. I lifted up my eyes in the depths of night, full of longing, to a woman. Ah, Satan's malice left me a beating heart to remind me of my torment. The dull glow I feel burning here, can I call it love, accursed being that I am? Ah, no! It is a longing for redemption [Jewish egoism, inability to love] that might be bestowed on me through an angel like this."

Senta: "He stands before me, his features full of suffering." She feels "the anguish that burns within my breast." Salvation "might be bestowed on you, poor being, through me." [Senta, in contrast to the Dutchman, feels pity.]

The Dutchman now asks her directly whether she will comply with her father's wishes and [according to Wagner and Hitler: characteristic for a Jew]: "After a life of torment, shall I find in your faithfulness my long-sought peace?" Senta answers: "I will always be obedient to my father."

Dutchman: "So unconditionally? How could you have such deep compassion for my suffering? [The Jew doesn't understand this.] Ah, if I can still hope for redemption, let it be through her. Ah, if you sensed the fate you would then share with me [if you became a Jewess], it would warn you of the sacrifice you will be making for me, if you swear to be faithful to me. Your youth would shudder and flee from the lot you would bring upon yourself if you did not keep your vow of eternal faithfulness."

Senta reassures him: "To him to whom I vow it [faithfulness], I give one thing: faithfulness until death." Dutchman: "Hear, you powers that have repulsed me, I have found my salvation." [Jewish egoism]

Daland enters again and asks whether he may announce the betrothal of the two at the celebration that takes place each time his destroyer successfully returns. There are no objections, and he "gives his hand to this union." The Dutchman again immediately thinks only of himself: "Hell, you are mocked by her faithful love." [The attempt to be freed of one's sins through another person]

ACT III

The celebration at the port, on the pier between the destroyer and the high seas sailing ship. Girls bring drinks and food. Daland's sailors are with them. The Dutchman's crew doesn't appear and remains silent.

The chorus of sailors sings: "No sign of the crew. They are guarding their treasure like dragons." When the girls want to bring wine aboard the high seas sailing ship, the crew calls out, invisible, from inside the ship: "Black Captain, go ashore. Seven years are over; seek a blond maiden's hand! Blond [Aryan] maiden, be faithful to him. Bridegroom, ho, storm wind howls, bridal music, the ocean dances to it! Captain, are you here again? Set sail! Your bride, say, where is she? Off to sea, Captain, you have no luck in love! Blow, storm winds, howl! Leave our sails in peace! Satan [the Jewish demon] has blessed them, and they will not tear in all eternity!"

The sailors, women and girls are horrified and try to drown them out with their own singing. But the Dutchman's crew bursts out in loud, scornful laughter.

FINALE

Senta runs out of the crew's common room. Erik follows her and asks whether he has been wrong [about her]. Senta asks him to leave her alone. Erik: "Righteous God, what unholy power [The Jewish demon] led you astray? What power seduced you so quickly? Your father, he brought the bridegroom with him. I know him well. I can imagine what happened! But you gave your hand to a man who had barely crossed your threshold!"

Senta: "I must not see you again, nor think of you. A high duty commands it." [A higher duty demands this salvation.] No, she had not sworn eternal faithfulness to Erik back then. Erik: "Senta, do you deny it? With your arm entwined around my neck, did you not declare your love for me anew? The thrill I felt at the clasp of our hands, tell me, was that not the assurance of your true love?"

The Dutchman has overheard the couple and now approaches them: "Lost! Ah! Lost! Salvation is lost forever! Senta, farewell! Your vow of faithfulness is broken, as well as my salvation. I am driven to the sea again. [The wandering Jew] I doubt you! I doubt God. What you promised was a jest to you! Lost! Lost! Forever lost!"

"Hear of the fate from which I save you! I am doomed to the most horrible of lots: I would rather welcome death ten times over! [Ahasuerus damned by Jesus] Only a woman can free me from this curse, a woman who would be faithful to me until death. For know, unhappy girl, the fate that meets those who break their vow to me: Eternal damnation is their lot! Countless victims have paid this sentence through me! But you shall be saved! Farewell! Away, my salvation, forever. You do not know me, you do not suspect who I am! Ask the seas throughout the world, ask the seaman who has sailed the ocean; he knows this ship, the dread of all devout men: I am called the Flying Dutchman!"

He goes aboard his high sea sailing ship and sets out to sea immediately. Senta now swears that she will be faithful to him until death and jumps from a cliff into the sea, thus taking her own life. [Sacrificial death of a blond girl from the noble race]

At the premiere in 1843, Wagner's romantic opera ended here. In a later revision [1860], a repetition of the salvation motif was added after the hard musical ending.

The salvation motif

Senta and the Dutchman are seen in a close embrace rising from the water like a Fata Morgana. This version is now generally used on the stage, decisively altering the original and antisemitic conclusion of the work.

Curtain

6.3. *Tannhäuser und der Sängerkrieg auf Wartburg*
Tannhäuser and the Singers' Contest at Wartburg Castle

Beginning in 1933, Reichsführer SS Heinrich Himmler planned to set up an ideological center for his Schutzstaffel, his protection squadron, in the Wewelsburg, a castle in Westphalia. It was to be a kind of isolated, central site for training and meetings of the highest SS officers. Nordic symbols and ornaments draped the interior spaces of the Wewelsburg.

Himmler announced that he intended to hold annual meetings of the Gruppenführer – that is, gatherings of the highest ranking SS officers – at the Wewelsburg. Swearing-in ceremonies were also to take place here. The greater the power of the SS became in the German Reich, the more monumental the construction plans. A gigantic castle complex was to be created in the Wewelsburg, referred to as the "Reichshaus der SS-Gruppenführer." These plans were to be carried out by inmates of a concentration camp set up in Wewelsburg especially for this construction project. As of 1941, it ranked as an independent main camp, on an organizational level with Buchenwald, Sachsenhausen and Dachau.

More than 3,900 inmates of the concentration camp in Niederhagen-Wewelsburg were used for forced labor to carry out this and other construction projects. At least 1,285 people died there as a result of the work and detention conditions, as well as abuse and arbitrary actions on the part of the SS guards. However, the concentration camp in Wewelsburg was also a Gestapo execution site. At least 56 people were murdered on the camp grounds or on a separate SS firing range in the nearby woods. Structural remains of the Nazi architecture that have still been preserved are two rooms in the North Tower of the Wewelsburg, which are also part of the exhibition tour: the "Gruft" (Vault) and the "Obergruppenführersaal" (SS Generals' Hall). No substantiated data is available regarding their planned use. A floor ornament from this room, in stylized form, became an identification symbol in far-right circles all over the world beginning in the 1990s.

In his introduction to the Peters piano score of 1914, Richard Sternfeld (1858-1926) points out the antithesis seen in Wagner's *Tannhäuser*. This has to do with "depicting the contrast between the somber and sinister sensuality of the Venusberg and the bright spring world of Thuringia – the contrast between two domains depicted by all of Wagner's dramas – only by means of music." Richard Wagner may criticize the dogma of the Roman Catholic church, but he sees the true evil among the Jews, the "plastic demon of the fall of humanity." And in "Judentum in der Musik" (Jewishness in Music), he writes: "[Nevertheless,] instead of freeing [ourselves] from the bonds of this Christian despotism, we are sold to a much more evil mistress with all our being: Industry." This is the art, Wagner says, that now fills the entire world. Its essence is capitalism [Judaism, the luxurious and immoral Venusberg]. Its moral objective is show, profit.[5]

The apocalyptic final battle between Venus [Judaism] and Elisabeth [the Aryan race] in Wagner's opera is also seen by Hitler as a struggle between the mortal enemy and "parasites in the body of other peoples," the Jews and the Germanic race. This is why the enemy [Venus] has to be destroyed.[6]

Like the undogmatic Christianity in which Wagner embeds Tannhäuser, Hitler shows himself to be similarly nonconfessional in judging the "Jewish-materialistic spirit": "I believe that I am acting in the spirit of the almighty Creator today: By warding off the Jews, I am fighting for the work of the Lord." [7]

---

[5] Peter Bendixen and Bernd Weikl, *Einführung in die Kultur- und Kunstökonomie, 3rd edition* (Wiesbaden, 2011).
[6] Hans-Ulrich Wehler, *Der Nationalsozialismus: Bewegung, Führerschaft, Verbrechen 1919-1945* (Munich, 2009).
[7] Saul Friedländer, *Nachdenken über den Holocaust* (Munich, 2007).

Characters:

- Hermann, Landgrave of Thuringia
- Tannhäuser
- Wolfram von Eschenbach
- Walter von der Vogelweide
- Biterolf
- Heinrich der Schreiber
- Reinmar von Zweter
- Elisabeth, niece of the Landgrave
- Venus
- A young shepherd
- Squires, chorus, dancers and extras

Time and place: 1933, Wewelsburg Castle

Wewelsburg Castle

ACT I

First scene: The Venusberg

Wagner himself provided detailed stage directions and set suggestions for this opera: A shimmering blue lake is to stretch out in the background. Bathing in it are naiads, water nymphs from Greek mythology. Sirens are reclining on the shore. Venus is lying there, and Tannhäuser has his head on her lap.

The grotto is immersed in rosy light [Red light district, brothel]. The nymphs are dancing [Pole dancing] and couples openly make love. [Swinger club run by Jews?] Wagner wants tumultuous, wild and immoral passion, in contrast to the chaste, decent and noble world of the Aryan race.

In the second scene, Tannhäuser suddenly grasps the fact that, as a representative of the noble race, he cannot remain here in the midst of the immoral depravity of the lower race: "I cannot measure the time I have tarried here! Days, moons no longer exist for me, for I no longer see the sun, nor the friendly stars of heaven. I no longer see the blades which turn freshly green and bring the new summer. I no longer hear the nightingale that proclaims the spring. I must flee from your kingdom. Let me go!" Yet Venus uses all the means at her disposal, be they erotic or immoral, to try to further bind him to her. "Beloved, come! See the grotto over there, filled with mild, rosy fragrance! That abode of the sweetest delights would enchant even a god!"

But Tannhäuser decides to flee from this grotto of lust and turns to Christianity, declaring: "My salvation lies in Mary!" At that, Venus cries out and collapses. [Using Christianity as a weapon against Judaism was always crucial for Hitler, too.] In the third scene, Tannhäuser ascertains: "Ah, the burden of sin weighs heavily upon me." In the fourth scene, he confirms: "No, I may never look back." He encounters his friends, including the Landgrave, and wants to join the NSDAP again.

ACT II

Festival Hall in the Wewelsburg

Wewelsburg: SS Generals' Hall

y also into his apocalyptic vision. According to God's plan, Landgrave, meet. The two had secretly been the perfect couple before Tannhäuser departed for the Jewish Venus and her brothel. The duet the two share is an overpowering proof of their love: "Praised be the hour, praised be the power! I will bravely dedicate myself to this new-found life. Trembling with joy, I call its fairest wonder mine." Elisabeth of the noble race again becomes the great love of the noble singer.

The Landgrave and his niece Elisabeth welcome the arriving guests. There are swastika flags. All the men are in gala Nazi uniforms. The chorus of knights and noblemen intones: "Joyfully we greet the noble hall, where art and peace may only dwell where the cry long resounds: Heil to Thuringia's prince, the Landgrave Hermann!" [This exultation clearly anticipates the exuberant calls of "Heil!" as they were later heard at the Reichsparteitagsgelände in Nuremberg or the Berliner Sportpalast].

The Landgrave announces the day's topic, understanding the true essence of love. Wolfram von Eschenbach is to begin. He greets the attendees: "What a glorious sight makes my heart glow! So many heroes, brave, German and wise – a proud forest of oaks, magnificent, fresh and green. And I see women, lovely and virtuous, delicate flowers of a richly-perfumed garland. My gaze is delirious from this sight, my song is silenced before such radiant charm." By no means does he wish for sexual relations, would not "taint the spring with sinful boldness," but rather "in prayer, I would practice devotion and gladly shed the last drop of my heart's blood. You nobles may gather from these words how I see the purest essence of love."

Tannhäuser can no longer bear this piety and willing sacrifice, the renouncement of physical love. He thinks back to the highly erotic time he spent with Venus, to the exquisite

"Rassenschande" [racial defilement], and makes clear to everyone present that he finds pleasure in that which is immoral and in the forfeiture of morals: "My song shall ring out to you, goddess of love; let me now loudly sing your praise! Your sweet allure is the source of all beauty, and every fair wonder stems from you! Only he who has known your passionate embrace, only he knows what love is! You poor beings who have never enjoyed her love – away, away to the Venusberg!"

All the listeners are horrified. The Waffen SS wants to liquidate Tannhäuser immediately. [Goebbels later punished "Blutschande" through sexual intercourse between Jews and Aryans with death.] Elisabeth throws herself between Tannhäuser and his attackers and pleads with all of them, including her uncle, the Landgrave, for clemency for the singer. Tannhäuser is spared for the moment, but must go on a pilgrimage to Rome, so that the Pope can absolve him of his sin.

ACT III

The Führerbau

A chorus of pilgrims draws near. Wolfram enters the Führerbau and discovers Elisabeth, who is praying before an image of the Virgin Mary. He sings of the "death in her heart" that Tannhäuser dealt to Elisabeth through his commitment to Venus and thus to the "Blutschande" – the racial defilement - in the second act.

"Prone, in searing pain," Elisabeth pleas just the same, day and night, for Tannhäuser's salvation, and thus shows the "eternal power of holy love!" [Wagner again anticipates components of the program of the National Socialists, in which a nondenominational "Germanic Positive Christianity," as opposed to the "Jewish materialistic spirit," is designated in the framework of the "sense of propriety and morality of the Germanic race."] Elisabeth stands up, wants to leave, and Wolfram tries to help her. She resists and leaves the stage.

Wolfram now sings the famous "Ode to the Evening Star." Tannhäuser suddenly appears, having returned from Rome.

The Führerbau

He reports to Wolfram in the "Romerzählung" [Rome narrative] that the Pope did not grant him absolution for his "Rassenschande," sex with a Jewish Venus, and cites the curse of the Pontifex: "If you have shared such sinful passions, and enflamed your lust at the fires of hell, if you have tarried at the Venusberg, then you are damned for eternity!"

After his failure in Rome, which means eternal damnation, Tannhäuser now wants nothing more than to return to the Venusberg, to the brothel: "I return to you, Venus, to the magical charms of your night. I descend into your court, where your charms will smile on me forever."

Tannhäuser summons Venus again: "Goddess, guide me!" And she appears with these words: "Welcome, unfaithful man! Do you seek love in my arms? The fountain of pleasure will flow forever for you. Oh, come! Be mine forever!"

But now Wolfram insistently relates to his friend that Elisabeth is praying for him in Heaven, and Tannhäuser grasps [too late] that Elisabeth has sacrificed herself for him. [Note the analogy: Senta also sacrifices herself for the Flying Dutchman.] The Pilgrim Choir crosses the stage again. The open casket with Elisabeth's body is carried in. Tannhäuser bends over it, dies, and Venus, as the embodiment of the Jewish race, collapses and is thus "eradicated." The Pilgrim Choir sings in the figurative sense of Wagner's salvation mythology, which also plays a major role in his antisemitic writings: "Heil! Heil! Heil to the miracle of mercy! Salvation is given to the world!"

Curtain

6.4. *Lohengrin*

As in *The Flying Dutchman* and *Tannhäuser* – and later in Parsifal – redemption, the nemesis of the inferior race in terms of the antisemitism of the Nazi era, is also a central motif in *Lohengrin*. "Elsa longs for the Savior, who will free her from a shameful suspicion [through the lower race], while Lohengrin longs for a woman whose love and devotion will free him from cold divinity and give him a life with warmth. But the divine demands absolute belief, and a woman's love demands total trust. This results in the tragic conflict that leads to the separation and destruction of the lovers. The means through which this unity is achieved is brilliant: The A major key for the Christian symbol of salvation, F sharp minor for its pagan adversary, Ortrud."[8]

There is no doubt that Richard Wagner wanted to point out these two worlds: The noble race of the masters [Elsa and Lohengrin] and the lower and criminal race of the Jewish subhumans (Ortrud and Friedrich von Telramund). Hitler and his friends recognized this and exploited it ideologically for the annihilation of the Jews.

Characters:

- Heinrich "The Fowler," German king
- Lohengrin
- Elsa of Brabant
- Friedrich von Telramund, Count of Brabant
- Ortrud, his wife
- A herald of the king
- Four nobles of Brabant
- Four pages
- Duke Gottfried, Elsa's brother
- Saxon and Thuringian counts and nobles
- Counts and nobles from Brabant
- Women's chorus and extras

Place and time: Berlin 1936

---

[8] See Richard Sternfeld's description of the plot in the introduction to the Peters Edition piano score.

Olympic Stadium, Berlin Olympic Park

ACT I

First scene

King Heinrich is holding an assembly of his military forces at the Berlin Olympic Park. The Saxon nobles and their military squads are sitting in the tiers on the left side, those from Brabant on the opposite side. The King greets the Brabantians and reports on the problems facing the kingdom: "Shall I first report to you on the tribulation so often wreaked on German soil from the east [The Bolshevik-Jewish enemy]? But it was I, head of the Reich, who had to contrive an end to such shameful humiliation. By victory in battle, I won peace for nine years [Hitler-Stalin Pact], and I used it for the defense of the Reich [military build-up]. I had fortified towns and castles built [Albert Speer's pompous buildings]. But now the truce is over, and the enemy is arming itself with savage threats. [Hitler: 'We have been returning fire.'] Now it is time to defend the

Reich's honor. East or west? That concerns everyone! [Goebbels: 'Do you want total war?'] Wherever there is German soil, raise troops of fighters [Mobilization]: Then no one shall ever dare insult our German Reich again." [Hitler's speech against Jewry and its efforts to achieve world domination.]There is discord among the Brabantians because they have no ruler, the King now laments. He wants to hear the reason for this from Friedrich von Telramund. He reports of the death of the Duke of Brabant and says that he had been given the duty of caring for his children, Elsa and Gottfried. The Duke had also promised that his daughter Elsa would be his wife. She, however, had murdered her brother, Gottfried. Therefore Telramund did not marry Elsa, but Ortrud, the daughter of the Duke of the Frisians, Radbod, and now, before the King, he accuses Elsa of murdering Gottfried, her brother. She did so, he says, in order to lay claim to the throne for herself, in order to be in a position to refuse to marry him — Telramund — and then to enter into a different, secret relationship.

Second scene

The King has summoned Elsa, and she appears "radiant and pure!" In *The Flying Dutchman*, Senta becomes engrossed in the picture of the Dutchman and sings the ballade of his pitiable fate, from which she wants to offer him salvation. Elsa now tells of her dream: "In the light of his shining armor, a knight approached. I had never before seen a man of such purity of virtue. A golden horn at his hip, leaning on his sword, he thus came out of nowhere to me, this worthy knight. With courteous bearing, he gave me consolation. I will wait for this knight. He shall be my champion!" [The Führer, Hitler]

Elsa has now admitted to having a secret admirer, argues Telramund, and insists on his accusation, for which he claims to have witnesses. He is also willing to duel to prove his honor. The King therefore suggests a so-called ordeal by combat. But Elsa insists on her vision and begins again: "I will wait for this knight; he shall be my champion! Hear the reward I offer to the man sent by God: He will wear the crown in my father's domains. I shall consider myself happy if he accepts my possessions. If he wishes to make me his bride, I will give myself to him completely." The Herald now calls out to the group several times, asking for a volunteer who is willing to fight against Friedrich von Telramund.

Third scene

Lohengrin [The Führer] appears. He is standing in an amphibian vehicle with wheels that is pulled by a machine in the form of a white swan, connected with a golden chain. The vehicle slowly rolls to the middle of the Olympic Stadium. Lohengrin appears as a mystical, divine figure with shining weapons and is greeted by everyone as an incredible miracle, as a man "sent by God." He steps out of the vehicle and sends it away: "I thank you, my dear swan." He approaches the King, who asks him whether he has been sent by God. [This is reminiscent of Heinrich Himmler, the Wewelsburg, and the Führer cult. Just as Lohengrin came from the Castle of the Holy Grail to save people in need, the good aspects of the Nazi ideology came from the Wewelsburg.]

Lohengrin now explains that he has come to fight for a young, innocent woman [To defend what is noble against that which is demonic, evil, Jewish]. If I am victorious, he asks Elsa, will you marry me? She wants nothing more than that. However – this is Lohengrin's condition – she may never know who he is or where he comes from: "You must never ask me."

He declares his love, and she promises to marry him. The bystanders are overwhelmed by this positive course of events and manifest this by calling out "Heil!" [The Nazi greeting]. Lohengrin says that Elsa is innocent and calls Telramund a liar. The duel, the ordeal by combat, will prove it. Now those present advise Telramund not to compete with this divine figure, but he stands by his accusation of Elsa and says that he has not lied. The two begin their duel. Lohengrin attacks first. Wagner's score indicates the moment the sword is thrust and Telramund falls to the ground. Lohengrin: "Through God's victory, your life is now in my hands. I will spare it. May you devote it to repentance!" [The greatness, the nobility of the heroic Aryan figure]

All of the participants are exultant about this very positive outcome and the fact that Elsa has been proven innocent: "Victory, victory, heil." Elsa throws herself on Lohengrin's breast: "To complete my joy, take all that I am!" Ortrud stares at Lohengrin with a black look: "Who is it who defeated him [Telramund], through whom I [The lower race, Jewry] am powerless?" [through the noble master race: Hitler destroys Jewry]. Friedrich von Telramund sinks to the ground, unconscious, and the chorus increases its cheers of "Heil!" for Lohengrin [Exactly as the Führer was saluted].

ACT II

The Great Hall

The "Grosse Halle" (Great Hall) in Berlin (Germania), planned by Rüstungs-minister (Minister of Armaments) and architect Albert Speer (1905-1981) and Hitler. It was never built.

First scene

Telramund and Ortrud on the steps before the entrance: In the meanwhile, the King has declared Telramund to be an outcast. No one is permitted to help him or to come close to him. "Wherever I turn, I am condemned. Through you, Ortrud [The Jewess], I have had to lose my honor, my glory. Would that I had chosen death, for I am so wretched!" [He who associates with Jews] And to Ortrud: "Was it not your idea to accuse the innocent Elsa [From the noble race]? Did you not lie to me, that you saw the crime being carried out?

How Elsa herself drowned her brother there in the pond? Did you not thus induce me to renounce the hand of the innocent Elsa and take you as my wife, because you were Radbod's last descendant?" He continues: "And did you not make me a shameful accomplice to your lie, and did God not pass judgment on me for this and strike me down?"

Ortrud counters: "You call your cowardice God." This Christian God is weak: "Give me the power, and I will easily show you what a weak God it is that protects him [Lohengrin]." Ortrud draws Telramund to her: "Sit here beside me! The hour has come for me as a seer to enlighten you!" Lohengrin only won through magic, not through God, and thus deluded the court. The idea would be to induce Elsa, despite her promise, to ask Lohengrin where he comes from and who he is. Telramund is now convinced that he can free himself from his predicament by this ruse and thereby reinstate his honor. This is followed by a short duet by the two conspirators: "May the act of vengeance be borne out of the stormy night of my bosom! Know, you who are lost in sweet sleep [Elsa and Lohengrin], that disaster awaits you!" [The treachery and falseness of the lower race]

Second scene

The door to a side entrance to the Great Hall opens from the inside, and Elsa comes out. With her light-colored clothing, in contrast to Ortrud's black attire, she can immediately be recognized as a member of the pure, noble race. Ortrud addresses Elsa and gives her the blame for Telramund's and her own misery. Elsa feels compassion for them. [The higher race can feel pity.] "How poorly would I value your benevolence, Almighty One, who has so favored me [through Lohengrin's love], if I were to cast aside the misfortune of the one who kneels in the dust before me [pity for the pleading Ortrud]. Oh, never! Ortrud! Wait for me! I myself will let you in." Elsa goes back into the Great Hall. Ortrud stays and asks her gods for help: "Bless my deception and hypocrisy, so that my revenge may be successful!" [The Jewish demon]

Elsa opens the main entrance to the Great Hall for Ortrud and lets Ortrud join her inside. Elsa: "My heart wants to stop beating when I see you so humbled near me! Stand up! Oh spare me your supplications! If you hated me, I forgive you. For what you have already suffered through me, I beg you to forgive me, too!" Elsa says that her husband Lohengrin will forgive Telramund as well at the wedding planned for the next day [Again the greatness and nobility of the Aryan race].

Ortrud now speaks of her power to recognize things that others do not see and offers her help to Elsa. She would like to look into Elsa's future and asks whether she knows what magic has brought the unknown knight to her. "Couldn't you imagine, with the mysterious ways of this man: May he never leave you as he came to you, through magic!" At first, Elsa is startled and turns away, but – according to Wagner – she then turns to Ortrud again, full of sorrow and compassion: "Poor woman, you can never imagine that my heart can love without any doubts? You have indeed never known the happiness that only comes through faith? Let me teach you how sweet the bliss of perfect trust is! Let yourself be converted to faith. A happiness exists without regret!" Ortrud says to herself: "This pride will teach me how to undermine her faithfulness. I will turn her own weapon against it. Her pain will yet come through her pride!"

Elsa now leads Ortrud into the bower. Telramund, who has heard the conversation of the two women, senses that evil will come to pass: "Evil is thus entering this house! Oh woman, fulfill what your cunning has devised. I do not have the power to hinder your plan! The disaster began with my defeat. Now let them fall who brought me to it! Only one thing do I see before me, urging me on: He who robbed my honor [Lohengrin] shall be destroyed!"

Third scene

All of the gates to the Great Hall are opened. The chorus appears on the large square in front of the hall: "The day promises much. The noble hero who wrought such great miracles may perform more wondrous deeds." The Herald proclaims that Friedrich von Telramund has been sentenced to moral excommunication and is therefore to be ostracized, which the chorus is pleased to hear. The herald then announces the planned marriage of Elsa and the unknown hero and the fact that the King will grant him the land and crown of Brabant. The blond hero does not want to be called the Duke, but the Protector of Brabant. [Similarly, Hitler was not the Kaiser, but Führer, and thus Protector of the German Reich.] The crowd answers: "Heil to the Protector!" [An especially clear reference to Hitler and the then current: "Heil to the Führer!"]

In the name of the Protector of Brabant, the Herald invites everyone to the wedding celebration to take place that day and to the military campaign to the east the next day. Four nobles come forward and question whether such a war is right: "Against an enemy who has never yet threatened us? [Hitler's invasion of Poland] Such bold beginnings should not be granted to him! Who will stop him [Lohengrin, here the Protector] if he gives the order?"

Telramund steps into the middle, saying: "I will" and accuses Lohengrin of perjury during the ordeal by combat. These four nobles and Telramund now hide. Four pages enter and prepare a path for the participants and for Elsa.

Fourth scene

The ceremonial wedding procession leads from the entrance to the Great Hall down the steps to the middle and crosses the square to the lefthand hall, to the Führer's Palace, which was planned by Albert Speer, but also never built. The wedding ceremony is to take place there. Right in front of the entrance, Ortrud suddenly stands in front of Elsa and insists that she should defer to her.

Führer's Palace

It is wrong that she should be treated like a servant; Elsa should bow before her: "Although false judgment caused my husband [Telramund] to be banished, his name was highly honored throughout the land. He was respected for his great virtue, and his brave sword was known and feared. But yours, who knows him here? You cannot even utter his name. Can you tell us whether his lineage, his nobility are certain? When he will leave again, and for where?" This would obviously cause problems for him, which is why he has forbidden you to ask about his background and his name.

Ortrud presses Elsa more and more, as if everyone present were of the opinion that the stranger were a criminal. Elsa regrets having fallen for her hypocrisy. Ortrud keeps insisting as to whether Elsa could utter the name and the lineage of the stranger and whether it would cause problems for him if he were identified. [The evil nature of the Jewess] Elsa: "You slanderer! Heinous woman! This exalted man is so pure and noble, so virtuous, that whoever dares to doubt his mission will never be free from ill fortune. [Loyalty to the Führer]. Did not my dear hero, with God's help, strike down your husband in combat? Now you should all say, according to the law, which one of the two can be innocent?" Ortrud answers: "Your hero's innocence would quickly be tarnished if he were forced to tell of the magic that gives him such power here! If you do not dare to ask him, we all have reason to believe that you yourself are worried that his innocence may not be what it seems!"

Fifth scene

The King, Lohengrin, the counts and the nobles appear. Their procession is disturbed by a commotion in the foreground. Elsa rushes over to Lohengrin, very excited. The King: "What is this dispute?" Lohengrin: "What do I see? That miserable woman is near you?" Elsa asks him to protect her from Ortrud and explains that she had only taken her in out of pity and that she had trusted her too much. Lohengrin addresses Ortrud: "You dreadful woman, get away from her!" And he asks Elsa whether Ortrud had poisoned her heart.

Suddenly Telramund comes out of his hiding place and tells the King in a passionate accusation of Lohengrin that the ordeal by combat had been false. "He whom I see standing radiantly before me [Lohengrin – Hitler], I accuse him of magic! May the power he won through trickery be scattered like dust before God's breath [From a private to Führer through the seizure of power]. The stranger conceals his name and his lineage and has fooled everyone through guileful magic: Now let him answer the charge. If he can, then I have been rightly punished; if not, you should see that his innocence has no basis!" Lohengrin accuses Telramund of being dishonorable and claims that he therefore must not answer.

Telramund brings the King into play. The stranger must reveal to him who he is. But Lohengrin refuses: "Yes, I can even refuse the King, as well as the highest assembly of all princes! Doubt will not burden them, for they saw my good deed! There is only one person to whom I must answer: Elsa!" He notices her uncertainty and expresses this in the quintet that follows: "Has the lying tongue of hatred taken her in?" His suspicion is justified. Elsa is struggling with herself: "What he conceals would cause him danger if he revealed it here before everyone. I would betray him if it were revealed here! If I knew his fate, I would keep the secret! Yet I have doubt in the depths of my heart!"

The King intervenes and tries to convince the stranger that it would be better to identify himself. But Lohengrin remains firm: "You heroes should not regret your faith [in Hitler], even if my name and origin are never made known." In the meanwhile, Telramund whispers secretly to Elsa: "Trust me! Let me tell you a way to obtain certainty! Let me wrest off a tiny part of him, just the tip of his finger, and I swear to you that you shall clearly see before you what he is hiding from you. I shall be near you tonight. Just call, and it will be done quickly without harm!" [Hitler's family history was kept secret or sugarcoated at the time. It was then said that the conspiracies and murders planned against him, the Lohengrin, the "heroic figure" of National Socialism, were thwarted by a higher power.]

Lohengrin says to them, "Away from her [Elsa], accursed ones [Ortrud and Friedrich]! Let me never again see you near her!" and thus puts the two of them in their places. And to Elsa: "In your hand, in your loyalty, lies the safeguarding of all our happiness! Does the power of doubt not leave you in peace? Do you wish to put the question to me?" Elsa calls him her savior and says that her love for him is greater than any doubt. The chorus adds their calls of "Heil!" and everyone turns toward the entrance to the Führer's palace and thus to the marriage ceremony.

ACT III

First scene: The nuptial chamber, a room in the Great Hall

The guests sing the world-known wedding march "Treulich geführt" [Here comes the bride] and accompany Elsa and Lohengrin through the door of the Führer's Palace into the open space. Then the two of them are led toward the High Hall and the bower. There they are at first alone as bride and groom.

Second scene

Elsa and Lohengrin assure each other of how of unique their love is, but suddenly Elsa mentions Lohengrin's secret: "Oh make me proud through your confidence that I may not wither in unworthiness! Let me know your secret, that I may clearly see who you are!" Lohengrin asks her to remain silent, but she insists more and more. He demands her complete trust. Even the King's crown would be too little to exchange for his origins of splendor and joy. Elsa cannot resist anymore. [The poison of the Jewish Ortrud is having its effect.] "Nothing can give me peace, nothing can remove my madness – other than, even if it should cost my life, to know who you are. Tell me your name! Where do you come from? What is your lineage?" Lohengrin: "Pity us. What have you done?"

Telramund has snuck in to kill Lohengrin [Attempt to assassinate the Führer]. Elsa quickly hands her bridegroom the sword, and the Aryan kills the Jew with it. He places Elsa, who has fainted, on the bridal bed and gives the nobles the order to bring the dead man to the King. There Elsa should learn who he is and where he comes from.

Third scene

The Olympic Park or the Reich Sport Field. Nobles and the entourage enter. The King addresses them and then asks: "Where is he now whom God sent for the glory and greatness of Brabant [Hitler]?"

Elsa is led in. The King looks at her with concern. Lohengrin walks onto the Sport Field and is greeted by the King: "Welcome, beloved hero! Those whom you so faithfully called to battle, they await you, eager to do combat under your leadership, certain of victory [against the Bolshevik-Jewish enemy in the east]." Lohengrin answers: "I cannot lead the brave heroes I summoned into battle." He did not come here to battle at their side. They should now hear him as a plaintiff. He reports that Telramund attacked him in the bridal chamber and whether it was not right that he killed him. "Secondly, you should hear another charge – that the woman whom God gave to me let herself be tricked into betraying me. You all heard her promise me that she would never ask who I am. But now she has broken her solemn oath and given her heart to perfidious counsel [from Ortrud and Telramund]. So hear now whether I am not equal in nobility to any of you."

This is followed by the famous Grail narrative, whose content is related to Wagner's final work, *Parsifal.* Lohengrin speaks of the Grail, of the vessel in the Castle of Monsalvat that is revered as a sacred relic with wondrous powers. Every year, a dove descends from Heaven to renew its magical powers. To those that serve the Grail, its content gives supernatural powers so that they can avoid evil and fight for virtue. However, the knights of this fraternity must remain unrecognized. This is why no one may question their actions, as otherwise they must return to Monsalvat. "I was sent to you by the Grail. My father Parsifal wears its crown. I am its knight. Lohengrin is my name." He again reproaches Elsa for not having trusted him, declares his love for her anew, and says that he now must "be parted from her."

Turning to the King again: "But, great King! Let me prophesy for you: Oh pure one, you will have a great victory! Not even in the most distant future will the hordes from the east be victorious over Germany." [Again: Wagner's Lohengrin already anticipates Hitler's campaign to the east, the Bolshevik-Jewish world domination. The plot in Lohengrin uses the Führer as an example and a challenge.]

Change of scene to the Olympic Stadium: Lohengrin's vehicle appears again. But now the swan is transformed into a dove, which is to pull the wagon away with him. Before that happens, Gottfried, Elsa's brother, emerges from the swan and is greeted as the new Duke of Brabant. Elsa collapses, and the Jewish Ortrud dies. [That which is noble and Germanic is thereby victorious over the demonic lower race of the Jews.]

Curtain

6.5. *Die Meistersinger von Nürnberg*
The Mastersingers of Nuremberg

On the occasion of the Reichsparteitag in 1937, a gala performance of Die *Meistersinger von Nürnberg* was given at the Nuremberg Opera House in the presence of the "Führer." A few months later, in 1938, the zealous Jew-hater and Gauleiter Julius Streicher had the synagogue on Hans-Sachs-Platz destroyed with the words of Hans Sachs from the gala opera: "Fanget an" (Let us begin).

Nurnberg Synagogue

Characters:

- Hans Sachs, cobbler
- Veit Pogner, goldsmith
- Kunz Vogelgesang, furrier
- Konrad Nachtigall, tinsmith
- Sixtus Beckmesser, town clerk
- Fritz Kothner, baker
- Balthasar Zorn, pewterer
- Ulrich Eisslinger, grocer
- Augustin Moser, tailor
- Hermann Ortel, soapboiler
- Hans Schwarz, stocking weaver
- Hans Foltz, coppersmith

- Walther von Stolzing, a young knight from Franconia
- David, apprentice to Sachs
- Eva, Pogner's daughter
- Magdalene, Eva's friend who helps in Pogner's household
- A night watchman
- Chorus, dancers, extras

Place and time: Nuremberg, 1937

ACT I

Wagner's – and Hitler's – heroic figure, the knight Walther von Stolzing, learns of the promise made by the goldsmith Pogner that, in addition to "all his possessions," he has offered his daughter as an additional prize for the singing contest to be held by the Masters. This means that she must marry the winner.

The blond, pure Aryan knight immediately wants to take part in the "trial," a kind of audition, in order to gain permission to participate in the singing contest. He wants to and must win the prize – Eva – by singing. David, the apprentice of the master cobbler Hans Sachs, is supposed to teach him the singing regulations, the so-called "table of rules."

Festive Opening Night

Hans Sachs' apprentices – some of them in the Hitler Jugend – are setting up the "marker's box,"[9] as well as a table with one or two small flags and swastikas. A table with a chair behind a curtain will be the place where Beckmesser, serving as the "marker" or judge, will sit. He won't be able

---

[9] The marker's box (Gemerk) is an altered chair with a curtain behind which the critic sits.

to see the singers, but is supposed to hear them and criticize them by making chalk marks on a slate. At the same time, David is reciting dozens of rules to Stolzing, which this Aryan has never heard of and does not understand.

The Mastersingers enter, three or four in Nazi uniforms, giving the Hitler salute. Pogner and Beckmesser talk about the planned contest. Beckmesser, the town clerk, appears, intentionally dressed fully in Nazi garb, to hide the fact that he is Jewish. [As a prototype for the town clerk Beckmesser, highly respected in Nuremberg, one might use the family tree of chief ideologist Ernst Alfred Rosenberg. The "incriminating" documents regarding the possible Jewish background of the writer of *The Myth of the 20th Century* could not be found at that time or even up to the present. This question was primarily discussed after his election to the Reichstag in October 1930. Publicly it was said then that "not a drop of German blood" flowed in his veins.[10]] Beckmesser is against giving Eva the right of refusal, which her father had granted her, in case the winner of the contest is not to her liking. If she should refuse, however, she would not be permitted to marry anyone else.

Stolzing, an Aryan, approaches the goldsmith Pogner [and father of his secret sweetheart, Eva], with whom he had spoken the day before about the sale of a property. He declares to the delighted Pogner that he has come to Nuremberg primarily because of his love for traditional pure art. Beckmesser, the Jew, shows from the outset his dislike of the Aryan Stolzing.

---

[10] Kurt Pätzold and Manfred Weißbecker, *Stufen zum Galgen: Lebenswege vor den Nürnberger Urteilen* (Berlin, 2004)

A debate develops between Sachs and Beckmesser in which the critic definitively pleads for the very strictest adherence to the rules, bureaucracy, and suppressive lifestyle of the National Socialists, who are currently gaining in power and support. As a Jew, he exaggerates all of this, so that Hans Sachs actually begins to question his Aryan ancestry.

Then they go on to the next item, the trial – that is, the audition. Pogner asks Stolzing to come forward again. The singer has to submit to a complicated, bureaucratic questioning, and he is only permitted to sing because Pogner insists. Since he has selected love as his theme, that is, not a topic from the Old Testament, Beckmesser is the responsible critic and is to take his place behind the curtain. Beckmesser thus becomes the marker, and he decides on the petition of the blond knight.

Stolzing's song is free, romantic, but by no means "degenerate art." His song is torn apart by Beckmesser's scratching chalk marks on the slate.

The secret Jew, Beckmesser, criticizes this "pure" art, since he [See Wagner] is against it, even hostile. [See Wagner's "Jewishness in Music."] He conducts these "proceedings" against the Aryan Stolzing with relentless harshness and subtracts point after point.

Walther von Stolzing: Part of the first verse at his trial as an example of a German, "Aryan" song

An argument develops between Beckmesser and Hans Sachs, in which Wagner caricatures the former through the musical structure and a Yiddish-like accent. Beckmesser complains to the cobbler Sachs about the poor work he did on his shoes.

Beckmesser with "Yiddish" expression in language and tone.

Beckmesser manipulates the other masters until, one by one, all of them agree with him. They decide: "Up, Masters, vote and raise your hands! Sung poorly and lost your chance!" And the blond singer is physically thrown out.

ACT II

It is the evening before St. John's Day, June 23rd. Magdalene, Eva's friend, asks her secret sweetheart, David, Hans Sachs' apprentice, whether the knight Stolzing has been successful in his trial, but David must tell her that he was not. Hans Sachs appears and tells his apprentice to bring parts of the workshop outside for the evening.

In the meantime, Pogner talks to his daughter Eva, who also hears from him that the blond Aryan has failed. She decides to ask Sachs for advice and help and to pay a visit to him. In the evening, on the street in front of his house, in his famous "Lilacs Monologue," he muses about the blond knight's song and what was new in it, as well as the purely fascist view of art: "The bird that sang today [The heroic figure, Stolzing] has a well-formed beak. He who hears him, and imagines he is imitating the bird, would be met with derision and disgrace."

Richard Wagner writes in "Jewishness in Music": "Only in real life can we regain the spirit of art, and not within its carcass, eaten up by worms [the Jews]." See also Hans Sachs in Act III: "… and they plant foreign aura with foreign baubles [the Jews, here Meyerbeer, Mendelssohn, etc., for example] in our German land. People would no longer know what is German and true. Honor your German Masters! And let the holy German art remain unchanged!" Cosima fulfilled this mandate in her own way: "We want German theater without Jews." Goebbels, as already noted above, stated in 1936: "We have German theater, German film, German press, German literature, German visual arts, German music, and German radio." In "Know Thyself" in 1881, Wagner himself summarizes this by remarking that the Jews are unable to originate any true culture, that the Jewish instinct bars any ideality."

Understandably fearful of being won in the song contest on the town commons by a singer like Beckmesser, Eva decides to offer herself as a bride to her fatherly friend, the widowed master cobbler. But Hans Sachs finally turns down her offer, thus overcoming his own midlife crisis. He is too old, he says – most unfortunately – and goes back into his house. The town crier reaches the stage, sings the first verse and thus half of his entire but always extremely impressive and important role, and leaves again, blowing his horn.

The sweethearts, the aristocratic, blond knight and the goldsmith's Aryan daughter, want to flee. Sachs shines his lantern out of the window and stops them. Rather strident lute strumming of a "degenerate art" is heard. Stolzing and Eva hide. Beckmesser, exaggeratedly conformist in Bavarian lederhosen, appears with his lute. Sachs, who has secretly been expecting the town clerk here, begins to bang on a piece of wood with powerful blows of the hammer. As loud as he can, he sings about a certain Eva. He doesn't want Beckmesser to be able to try to climb through Eva's window or even to be successful in serenading Pogner's daughter.

Finally Beckmesser, the secret Jew, asks the cobbler to have pity on him and to please stop hammering. Instead, if absolutely necessary, he should serve as the marker, the critic, for him. Suddenly the roles are reversed. Beckmesser says to Sachs: "Not with the hammer on the last... With chalk, please. Soft chalk." Sachs agrees, but insists on hammering. Sixtus Beckmesser sings off key, strums incorrectly. As a Jew, he has no feeling for pure, noble nature. Sachs marks his errors with loud, hard strokes on the wooden last. Beckmesser is rejected and thus – like "everyone who is rejected in Wagner's work" – becomes a "Jewish caricature" in line with Theodor Adorno.[11]

This noise wakes up the entire neighborhood. An unsettled, threatening atmosphere develops, with flashing lights, clinking windows, and the feeling of a pogrom. A Nazi demonstration marches across the stage. Flags with swastikas and other Nazi emblems can be vaguely seen.

David goes after the Jew Beckmesser in the dark. Most of the people, in nightclothes and some with Nazi accessories, move as a turbulent mass. Jews with Stars of David can be dimly recognized. They are treated brutally and led away.

---

[11] Matthias Küntzel, "Wagner war Avantgarde – als Musiker und Antisemit," *Die Welt*, April 28, 2013.

ACT III

This act is divided into Part I (The cobbler's workshop – Sachs' living room and workshop) and Part II (The town common), where a few Nazi flags, etc., have been set up in preparation for the singing contest which is to take place.

Part I: Sachs is sitting at his desk and is reading Rosenberg's *The Myth of the 20th Century*. It takes a while for him to notice his apprentice and tells him to change his clothes for the event that is going to take place on the Festwiese, a meadow outside the city. David leaves the stage, and Hans Sachs begins the famous "Madness Monologue." He hangs a large photo of Hitler on the wall and opens the window. The city of the Reichsparteitage is seen. The cobbler sings: "How peaceful, true to our customs, content in deed and work, my dear Nuremberg lies in the middle of Germany! ... Now let us see how Hans Sachs can weave this madness and perform a more noble work. For if it won't leave us in peace, even here in Nuremberg, a deed like this can rarely succeed without wily steps, and never without a bit of madness." [Wagner anticipates here the work of Hitler's Reichsparteitage in Nuremberg, among other things.] Hans Sachs takes a generous slug of Nuremberg Braunbier and drinks to the health of the Führer.

Stolzing has spent the night at Sachs' house. He now enters and tells of the wonderful dream he has had. Sachs wants to hear it and writes it down, while Stolzing invents the "Prize Song," totally in the style of Aryan art, that is, tonally – instead of "degenerate," or atonally – and sings it. (Here Wagner clearly demonstrates, by comparison with the song of the Aryan Walther von Stolzing, that Jews can only imitate an art that is so foreign to them.)

Hans Sachs and Stolzing leave to get dressed for the Fest-wiese.

The secret Jew Beckmesser sneaks into Sachs' living room, uninvited. At the end of a silent pantomime [Caricature of the hand-wringing Jew], he complains in a monologue about having been beaten. By chance, he discovers the Aryan Stolzing's Prize Song on the desk. The cobbler had left it lying there. Beckmesser puts it in his pocket. Sachs comes back, looking for the song, and is surprised by the unexpected visit. Beckmesser attacks him with furious speech and accusations. The critic blames Sachs for his unfortunate condition – his black eye, the broken lute, etc. – and finally charges him with wanting to participate in the song contest himself in order to win Eva. After all, he had proof: the song. Sachs simply gives it to him and denies that he had wanted to compete. He even permits the clerk to sing the song wherever he might want to, and however he thinks best.

Suddenly Beckmesser's attitude toward the cobbler poet changes completely. He has always thought he was the greatest, he says, always wanted to buy his goods, and is beside himself with joy and gratitude [Wagner: Jewish falsity]. Hans Sachs cautions him again that he should not mention to anyone that this song came from the cobbler. And Beckmesser swears that he will not do so [Jewish falsity]. He practically dances out of the shop.

Eva enters and says that her new shoes pinch her. The truth is that she is looking for her Walther, who has spent the night at Sachs' house. Stolzing appears. Sachs asks him for a third verse for the Prize Song. And the young noble sings his clear, pure melody with great enthusiasm. Now the cobbler has a bit of a temper tantrum, throwing half of the furnishings in the room around, and then explains to Eva that he had managed to successfully overcome his midlife crisis at the very last second. As he says, he did not want to act like King Marke did in *Tristan und Isolde*, who, being much too old, takes Isolde, who is much too young, because in the end it is indeed Tristan [here Stolzing] whom she wants, and so forth. Eva compliments Sachs and assures him that, if Stolzing hadn't existed, she would indeed have considered marrying him. Sachs calls Lene and David inside and begins to sing a blessing. He gives Walther's Prize Song a name: "The Morning Dream Song." The scene ends with a quintet, and the five soloists quickly leave the stage.

Quick scene change to the Nuremberg Reichsparteitagsgelände.

Nazi Party Rally Grounds

Part II: Nazi flags and other accessories on the Reichsparteitagsgelände. Many people have gathered, the guilds enter, and the "Girls from Fürth" [BDM – Union of German Girls] dance in the old German style. The Masters, in Nazi attire, climb onto their stands. Sachs arrives a little late and wants to hold his welcoming speech, but is prevented from doing so by the chorale. "Awake! Day is drawing near. I hear a blissful nightingale singing in the green grove, its voice ringing through mountains and valleys. Night is sinking in the west, while day begins in the east. The red glow of morning comes through the dark clouds."

It was not by accident that Richard Wagner used the original text by the historic Hans Sachs, in which he called Luther "die Wittenbergisch' Nachtigall (the Wittenberg Nightingale), that one now hears everywhere." Martin Luther's antisemitism is documented by his treatise "On the Jews and their Lies."

Here it is used as an homage to the figure of Hans Sachs [the composer Wagner himself]. It also anticipates a future "power" that is desired and is reminiscent of Wagner's political writings, the ideological bases for the nascent National Socialism. The demise of the Jews is expected to free "German" art from Jewish capitalism and egoism. Wagner further states clearly, although questioningly: "I cannot judge whether the decline of our culture can be stopped by a forcible expulsion of the subversive elements [the Jews], because powers are needed for this to occur whose existence I cannot confirm."

Hans Sachs is acclaimed by those around him, but he is not all that pleased about this. Deeply moved, he sings: "You make it easy for yourselves, but you make it hard for me. You give me, poor man, too much honor." At a moment in which he is not observed, Beckmesser tells Sachs that he is having problems with his song: "Oh, this song! I cannot make sense of it, though I've studied it long enough." [He is unable to understand it because he is a Jew.] The cobbler advises him to refrain from entering the song contest. But the town clerk still does so, though he is extremely nervous. He accentuates incorrectly, mixes up words, twists them and turns them around, and has not understood the meaning of the song.

Morgen ich leuchte in rosigem Schein von Blut und Duft

geht schnell die Luft; wohl bald gewon — — nen, wie zerron — — — nen,

im Garten lud — — — — ich ein garstig und fein

wohn ich erträglich im selbigen Raum, hol Geld und Frucht,

Bleisaft und Wucht.. mich holt am Pranger der Verlan — — — ger,

auf luftger Stei — — — — — ge kaum, häng ich am Baum.

Beckmesser's last appearance on stage

Those on the stage make fun of him: "A fine competitor! He will get his reward. He will soon hang from the gallows. We can see it now!"

As early as 1922, Hitler envisioned erecting a series of gallows on the Marienplatz in Munich. "Then the Jews will be hung, one after the other, and they will hang there until they stink." On December 18, 1941, Himmler noted in his duty calendar that, as he had requested, Hitler had confirmed the previous actions of the task forces and commanded: "Jewish question / Exterminate them as partisans."

Beckmesser accuses Sachs of having written the song. Now the latter must provide an explanation. He needs a witness for the fact that this composition did not originate with him and requests permission for the person to sing the song who actually created it and can now perform it without any errors. This is permitted. The blond Stolzing enters and sings the right words and endings, all in line with the National Socialist concept of art.

Beckmesser had totally distorted the song with his terrible rendering of it. He has thus betrayed himself as a Jew in line with Wagner's "Jewishness in Music." According to Wagner, German art is always foreign to the Jews. Now the Masters, the chorus and the extras carry in Nazi flags and put on armbands with the swastika emblem. Jews are beaten up. Beckmesser is stripped of his Nazi attire, so that a large Star of David becomes visible under it. Nazi thugs drag him from the stage. Stolzing and Eva are betrothed, and Sachs convinces everyone on the stage and in the audience in his great final address to them by celebrating holy German art, that which is "pure Aryan" art: "Beware! We are threatened by evil tricks. If the German people and the Reich should one day decay, under a false, foreign rule, soon no prince would understand his people. And they would plant foreign auras with foreign baubles in our German land. People would no longer know what is German and true, if it did not live with the honor of the German Masters. Therefore I say to you: Honor your German Masters! Then you will reject the evil spirits. And if you favor their works, even if the Holy Roman Empire should dissolve in mist, we would still have the Holy German Art."

The chorus praises Hans Sachs, alias Richard Wagner and Adolf Hitler, with: "Heil! Sachs! Nuremberg's dear Sachs!" [In 1924, the entire audience in Bayreuth stood up after the end of *Meistersinger* and sang several verses of the "Deutschlandlied." Calls of "Heil!" could also be heard.]

The master race of Aryans, as a "pure race," was to have the right to rise above the "impure race" of the Jews. Key phrases from Rosenberg's *The Myth of the 20th Century*: "The pride of the German people begins with its victory over everything that is low and greedy. A new youth is growing up in Germany in the service of German values, with a steel-hard will to atone for the event of November 9, 1918, and to shake off the foreign yoke. [The defeat in World

War One, also caused by the Jews] The National Socialists regard this formation of character as a core problem of our era…"

Goebbels now described the Jews as enemies of the people and parasites, and said that they would use their "right to hospitality" to cheat the German people and take advantage of them. So the German people had no other choice but to defend themselves against the mania of gold. Goebbels took advantage of the latent general antisemitism and referred to the destructive influence the Jews currently had, particularly in culture and art (See Richard Wagner]. Antisemitism – and not only as a means of propaganda – became a cruel weapon against the Jews. Hitler wrote on September 16, 1919: "If the Jew's feelings lie in the purely material, this is even more so in his thinking and striving … His actions will result in a racial tuberculosis of the peoples. And this is the result: Antisemitism based on purely emotional grounds will find its ultimate expression in the form of pogroms. An antisemitism based on reason, however, must lead to a methodical, legal suppression and elimination of the privileges of the Jews, which only they possess in contrast to other aliens living among us [Aliens Law]. The absolute ultimate objective, however, must be the complete and permanent elimination of the Jews. Both of these can only be achieved by a government with national power, never by a government with national powerlessness."

Curtain

6.6. *Der Ring des Nibelungen*
The Ring of the Nibelung

Der Ring des Nibelungen is Wagner's main work, and the one with which he inaugurated the Festspielhaus in Bayreuth in 1876. Pianist and music historian Cord Garben shortened this *Ring des Nibelungen* from four evenings and a total of sixteen hours to only seven hours. This version was presented at the Teatro Colón in Buenos Aires and is available on the market as a DVD. The following presentation is based on this score.

The mythological content is timeless and thus can also be applied to modern staging and set concepts. However, the public likes to anticipate archetypes, such as those that were very successfully shown in the hit "Lord of the Rings" as dreams for adults and children.

Characters:

- Alberich, an ugly dwarf
- Wellgunde, Rhinemaiden
- Flosshilde, Rhinemaiden
- Wotan, ruler of the gods
- Two giants, Fafner and Fasolt
- Freia, Wotan's sister-in-law
- Loge
- Mime, Alberich's brother
- Siegfried, Mime's foster son
- Siegmund and Sieglinde, twins
- Hunding
- Brünnhilde, Wotan's favorite daughter
- Fricka, Wotan's wife
- A forest bird
- Hagen, Alberich's son
- Gunther and Gutrune

In view of his Jewish, capitalistic attitude, his one-sided interest in profit, Alberich's capacity for love is diminished. The Rhinemaiden Wellgunde characterizes him this way: "Ugh, you hairy, vain dandy! Swarthy, horny, sulfurous dwarf!" Flosshilde is bothered by "his piercing gaze, his froglike figure, and his toadlike shape and croaking voice." The three Rhinemaidens finally laugh at Alberich: "In the shimmer of gold, how fair you do shine." [The ugly Jew with his unattractive voice]

Lust instead of love: lust can be bought [Jewish immorality]. Alberich tears the gold from the rock, to forge "the Ring of Revenge" and declares: "Thus I curse love!" [Wagner's characterization of the loveless Jew] Wotan, the father of the gods, has ordered the two giants, Fafner and Fasolt, to build a mighty castle for him. [Hitler and architect Albert Speer wanted to make "Germania" out of Berlin with their gigantic buildings, so they also used Wagner's idea here as a model. In the following example, Wotan already passes the idea on to the two National Socialists, Speer and Hitler.]

Wotan's castle has been built by the two giants. According to the contract, Freia, Wotan's sister-in-law, is to be given to them in payment for that work. She does not agree with this. Loge appears and tries to help. Wotan: "Loge, at last! Were you in such a hurry to correct the bad deal you made?" Loge replies: "What? What bad deal did I make?" Fricka speaks to her husband Wotan: "See what a deceptive rascal you trusted!"

Wotan's Castle Valhalla

The double-dealing Loge suggests a possible solution to the problem that might be considered: Alberich had unsuccessfully wooed the Rhinemaidens and then stolen the Rhinegold out of revenge. "He now deems it the dearest good, greater than a woman's grace." Fricka suggests that Wotan could fetch this gold, and the giant Fafner takes up this suggestion: "Wotan, hear what we have to say! Freia will remain in freedom, for I have found an easier payment. The red Nibelung gold will be enough for us rough giants." Wotan replies: "Have you lost your senses? Shameless ones, shall I give to you what I do not own?"

Alberich has piled up the stolen gold somewhere else, to forge the Ring from it. He goads the downtrodden Nibelungs on [Jewish exploitation]: "This way! That way! Hey! Hey! Ho! Ho! Lazy herd! Pile up the hoard there in heaps! Will you get going? Shameful folk! Mime, come to me! Rotten rascal! Get back to your bench and forge! Hey, get to work! Get down fast! Get gold for me from new shafts! Anyone who doesn't dig quickly will feel the whip! Mime will make sure that no one stands around idle, or else he shall scarcely escape the lashes of my whip!" Sinister commands describe Wagner's unpleasant Jewish characters.

The Ring represents power, which plays the most important role in the course of the story. The lower race, here Alberich, steals the Rhinegold, forges the Ring, and thus appropriates world domination. Alberich's character is the embodiment of exploitative capitalism, which was equivalent to Judaism for Wagner. George Bernard Shaw describes his impression: "What forces are there in the world to resist Alberic in his new character of sworn plutocrat? He is soon at work wielding the power of the gold. For his gain, hordes of his fellow creatures are thenceforth condemned to slave miserably, overground and underground, lashed to their work by the invisible whip of starvation. They never see him, any more than the victims of our 'dangerous trades' ever see the shareholders whose power is nevertheless everywhere, driving them to destruction. The very wealth they create with their labor becomes an additional force to impoverish them; for as fast as they make it, it slips from their hands into the hands of their master, and makes him mightier than ever. You can see the process for yourself in every civilized country today, where millions of people toil in want and disease to heap up more wealth for our Alberics. All this part of the story is frightfully real, frightfully present, frightfully modern; and its effects on our social life are so ghastly and ruinous that we no longer know enough of happiness to be upset by it."[12]

On January 30, 1939, a half year before the German invasion of Poland, out of which the Second World War developed, Hitler announced his plans for the genocide of the Jews in Europe during a speech at the Reichstag lasting several hours. "I have been a prophet very often in my life and was generally laughed at. During my struggle for power, it was primarily the Jewish people that merely laughed at my prophecies that one day I would lead the German nation and thus the entire people, and that I would then solve the Jewish problem, among many others. I believe that what was then roaring laughter on the part of the Jewry in Germany has in the meanwhile stuck in their throats. Let me be a prophet again today: If international financial Jewry within and outside of Europe should succeed in plunging the nations into a world war once again, the result would not be the Bolshevization of the world and thus the victory of Jewry, but rather the annihilation of the Jewish race in Europe." [13]

Alberich is everywhere, even in places where one doesn't expect to find him [the wandering Jew Ahasuerus].

At last, however, Wotan enters this agreement with the giants. Instead of Freia, they finally accept the gold, which is still in Alberich's hands. To ensure that Wotan will keep the promise, the giants take Freia along as a pawn. In the meantime, Alberich has forced his brother Mime to forge a Ring and a Tarnhelm — a magic helmet — out of the gold. After he has finished, Mime wants to wear these works of art himself and is whipped by his brother Alberich as punishment. Wotan and Loge appear at Alberich's place, and the latter brags about his powers, which he wants to use to conquer the world. [The Jews' power in the world was crit-

[12] George Bernard Shaw, *Ein Wagner Brevier. Kommentar zum Ring des Nibelungen* (Berlin, 1973).
[13] Hitler's Reichstag speech of January 30, 1939 (excerpt).

icized by Hitler.] Loge outwits Alberich. To demonstrate the magical powers of the Tarnhelm, Alberich first turns himself into a powerful dragon and then takes the form of a toad. Wotan and Loge tie him up and take the Tarnhelm from him.

In the following scene, Alberich is in Wotan's hands: "You have been captured, shackled by me, just as you imagined the world would already be in your power, with all in it that lives and moves. [Jewish domination] Now you need a ransom to free yourself." Wotan wants both the gold and the Tarnhelm. [Confiscation of Jewish property] To confuse things even more, Wotan also demands the Ring from Alberich, who finally gives him the treasure, while placing a terrible curse on it. [The curse of the Jewish Mammon] Alberich to Wotan: "Since it came to me with a curse, keep it now, guard it well! You will not escape my curse!" The giants then receive the gold and the Ring from Wotan and free Freia in exchange. They fight over the gold and the Ring. Fafner kills his brother Fasolt and takes both for himself.

The scene changes. Wotan and his wife Fricka behold their castle, full of joy. Wotan: "The castle glows resplendent, shining magnificently. In the morning sunshine, it shimmered unowned, proudly enticing me. [Confiscation of Jewish property] Follow me, woman! Dwell with me in Valhalla." And Loge, the visionary, looks after them: "They are hastening to their end, they who think themselves so strong and enduring. [The decline of the Thousand-Year Reich] I feel an enticing desire to transform myself into a flickering flame again – to burn those who once tamed me, rather than to foolishly die away with the blind, were they the most godlike of the gods. I want to think it over. Who knows what I will do!" [The end of the Aryan,

Germanic race through victory by the Bolshevist-Jewish enemies from the East.]

Exhausted, Siegmund seeks shelter in Hunding's dwelling. He and Hunding's wife, Sieglinde, are drawn to one another. Hunding comes home, sees this unknown guest, and notices a strong resemblance between his wife and this stranger. Hunding gives him shelter, but wants to know his name and where he comes from. When Siegmund tells them how tragic his life has been up to now and speaks of the kidnapping of his twin sister, whom he lost in the fight against a rival tribe, Hunding recognizes the man he had wanted to pursue, and whose sister is now his wife. Hunding challenges Siegmund to a duel the next morning and retires with Sieglinde. But Sieglinde signals to Siegmund that he should look at the trunk of the ash tree that is in the middle of the room. Siegmund remembers his father's prophecy, discovers the sword that he had hidden in the tree, and uses his superhuman powers to pull the weapon out of the trunk. In the meanwhile, Sieglinde has given Hunding a strong sleeping draft and comes back into the room to Siegmund.

He speaks: "My father promised me a sword. Winter storms have made way for springtime. So let the Wälsung blood flourish." The noble Teuton uses brilliant tones to sing his way into the hearts of his Sieglinde and the audience [and the National Socialist ideology of the Third Reich].

Wotan's favorite daughter, Brünnhilde, is supposed to intervene in the combat between Siegmund and Hunding and, according to Wotan's wish, make sure that Siegmund is victorious. Fricka, Wotan's wife, considers the incest between Siegmund and Sieglinde to be unforgivable and totally illegal. Wotan needs Siegmund, who is to recover the Ring for him. Yet his wife insists on adherence to the laws and thus on Hunding's victory in the coming duel.

Now Wotan talks to Brünnhilde, explains what has been happening, and retracts his order for her to help Siegmund. Brünnhilde speaks to Siegmund and describes the wonderful future he will have in Valhalla after his death. He will not agree to die if he cannot take Sieglinde with him, so he decides to kill the slumbering woman with his sword. Brünnhilde stops him, moved by such a great love, and – disregarding her orders – promises instead that she will protect the hero.

Siegmund and Hunding battle, and Wotan, who suddenly appears, breaks Siegmund's sword into pieces. Siegmund dies, and Brünnhilde takes possession of the broken sword. She quickly rides off with Sieglinde. And the father of the gods turns to Hunding: "Go to her, slave! Kneel before Fricka. Tell her that Wotan's spear has avenged that which caused her shame!" Now Hunding also dies on the spot. The heroic father is furious with his favorite daughter: "Woe to the guilty one! This impudent girl [Brünnhilde] will be punished terribly once my horse overtakes her in flight."

Six Valkyries await the arrival of their sister Brünnhilde. She asks them to help her and Sieglinde, as they are in great distress. She tells Sieglinde: "Make haste then, to the east. One thing you must know and always remember: You bear the world's greatest hero in your womb." She gives the pregnant woman the broken sword. [The world's greatest hero, Hitler, later hurries toward the east!]

The blond heroic figure, Siegfried, enters. He is the foster son of Alberich's brother Mime, who thus also belongs to the lower race. Siegfried has his bear chase Mime: "Eat him! Eat him, the ugly old smith. There are two of us, the better to tweak you. Bruin! Ask about the sword!" Mime is busy forging the broken sword, but Siegfried thinks the steel is not hard enough. He shatters it on the anvil and says to Mime: "When I see you standing, shuffling and slinking, buckling and nodding, blinking with your eyes, I want to grab you by your nodding neck and put an end to that nasty nix."

Mime replies that he received nothing but a broken sword from Siegfried's mother in exchange for providing food and shelter for the child. Siegfried wants this sword to be repaired immediately. He runs into the woods and leaves Mime back alone. Mime doesn't feel that he is capable of hardening the steel of the sword. Suddenly Siegfried comes back from the woods and says to Mime: "Hey there, you lazy rascal! Are you finally finished? Quick, how are you doing with the sword? Mime, you coward! Where are you?"

Mime explains that only someone who knows no fear would be able to forge this powerful sword, Nothung. Siegfried wants to experience the feeling of fear. Mime knows of a sleeping dragon, Fafner. And Siegfried wants to encounter him. "Quickly, then," Siegfried says to Mime, "make the sword." Mime explains that he is too weak to manage this, and Siegfried says: "This idler has ready ruses for me. He should admit that he is a bungler. Now he is cheating his way out with lies! Give me the pieces, and away with the bungler!" Now Siegfried gets to work himself. He forges the sword, and Mime enjoys imagining a cruel game: "The shimmering ring [The Ring] my brother [Alberich] made, to which he magically gave mighty powers, the shining gold that makes one a master, I have won it [The Ring], I rule over it." And against his own brother: Alberich himself, who once had me in bondage, I will now compel him to perform dwarf drudgery [as a slave]. I will go down there again as a Nibelung prince, and the whole host shall obey me. The world will kneel at my command, and they will tremble at my wrath. For truly, Mime will no longer have to toil. Others will win the eternal treasure for him. [The Jew has others work for him.] Hey! Mime, how did you do this! Who would have imagined this?" [Mime shows the false Jewish character Wagner and Hitler found so typical.]

The giant Fafner appears, now in the form of a huge dragon. Siegfried looks at him in amazement and clearly shows that he is not afraid of him. Finally he seriously wounds Fafner, but can still ask him about his origins. He also gives Siegfried information about the two giants. Fafner dies. Siegfried pulls the sword out of the dead giant's wound, and his blood flows over his hand. It burns like fire on his skin. He licks it off, and suddenly he can understand the language of the forest bird: "Hey! The Helmet and the Ring now belong to Siegfried! Oh, he must not trust the disloyal Mime! Siegfried must listen carefully to the rascal's hypocritical lies! He can understand what Mime is thinking in his heart, now that he has tasted the blood." [The warning against Mime, the falsity of Jewry]

Mime observes Siegfried: "He is thinking over how much the booty is worth. Now I will set a cunning trap, so that I can fool this stubborn child with friendly, false words." And he speaks directly to Siegfried: "Welcome, Siegfried. Did you slay the dragon? Wasn't he an awful fellow?" Because of the forest bird's remark, Siegfried doesn't fall for Mime's lie: "His death does indeed grieve me, as much more serious criminals still live and have not been slain. The one that had me murder him, I hate him more than the worm!"

Mime praises Siegfried with sugary falsehoods: "You have done what I needed you to do. Now I only need to recover the booty from you. I think I should succeed in doing so, for you are easy to fool. I must not delay removing you from my path. How else could I seize the booty, since Alberich is also after it?" He offers Siegfried something to drink: "Now, my Wälsung, you wolf's son! Drink, and choke yourself to death! You will never drink another swig." Siegfried lunges with the sword and – according to Wagner's staging comment – strikes a hefty blow to Mime, who immediately falls to the ground, dead. [Destruction of the Jew] Then Siegfried throws the corpse into the nearby cave and blocks the entrance with the body of the dead dragon.

Now that he can understand the language of the forest bird, he asks her for advice. After his negative experience with Mime [the Jew], he needs to find a noble companion. The forest bird tells him of the "most magnificent woman," who is sleeping on a high cliff, and: "Fire surrounds her abode." Anyone who can break through this ring of fire could awaken Brünnhilde and take her for his wife. Siegfried is thrilled: "Will I break through the fire? Can I awaken the bride?" He hears the voice of the forest bird: "A coward will never win the bride. Only he who knows no fear!" [The fearless, courageous, thus noble race]

Searching for Brünnhilde's wall of fire, Siegfried encounters Wotan, who confronts him in the form of the Wanderer. Siegfried tells him that he is searching for a rock on which a woman is sleeping, surrounded by a wall of fire. The Wanderer strongly advises him against continuing this search: "Fear the guardian of the rock! My power keeps the sleeping maiden enclosed. He who awakens her makes me powerless forever. He who desires this bride is faced by burning desire. Soon you will be devoured and consumed by an all-encompassing fire." Siegfried responds that he is not afraid of this fire, but the Wanderer now holds up his spear and blocks his way with it. Siegfried: "My father's enemy, I find you here? How glorious that I can now take revenge!" He strikes Wotan's spear. Wotan then picks up the pieces from the ground and disappears. He can no longer stop the hero, Siegfried, who finally breaks through the ring of fire and discovers Brünnhilde inside it. She wakes up: "Who is the hero who has awakened me?" He answers: "It is I, Siegfried, who has awakened you!"

Wagner comments: Both remain lost, full of resplendent rapture, upon seeing one another. [Hitler, the courageous Führer, undoubtedly saw himself as Siegfried, who "awakened" Brünnhilde, as the embodiment of Germany.]

In great vocal exultation, Siegfried and Brünnhilde avow their love. He repeats in brilliant, sustained tones: "Be mine! Be mine! Be mine!" And Brünnhilde answers him, with equal enthusiasm: "Oh, Siegfried! I have always been yours! I will always be yours!" [The frenetic celebration of Hitler, the savior of Germany] In a terrible vision, Brünnhilde proclaims: "Farewell, Valhalla's glowing world! Let your proud fortress crumble into dust. Farewell, resplendent glory of the gods! Dusk of the gods, let the darkness descend! Night of destruction, shroud us in mist. Radiant love, laughing death!" [Wagner's prophecy and

Hitler's longing for death? The demise of the Third Reich]
Brünnhilde throws herself into Siegfried's arms. After what
must have been a very profound night of love, Siegfried
gives the Ring to his Brünnhilde and receives from her
Grane, the horse that is now obedient to him. Again there
are sounds of jubilation: "Heil to you, Brünnhilde, resplendent star!" She joins in: "Heil to you, Siegfried, victorious light!" A repeated "Heil," each time with long, held
notes, from both of the protagonists, ends this scene. Siegfried sets off on a journey with the horse Grane.

Enthusiastic shouts of "Heil" accompanied National Socialism throughout the
twelve years of its existence. The usual greeting was: "Heil Hitler" or "Heil,
mein Führer." Hitler asserted repeatedly that Wagner was his religion. Here,
too, it is not difficult to ascertain how much he internalized Wagner's antisemitism and carried it out through the murder machinery of the Holocaust.

Siegfried meets Hagen, Alberich's son and thus also a member of the lower race. He tells him that he is not very interested in the gold of the Nibelung treasure and that he has
therefore left it behind in the cave. Siegfried has only taken
the Tarnhelm and the Ring with him. The latter, however,
he gave to Brünnhilde. Gutrune appears and serves a magic
drink to Siegfried, one that befogs the blond warrior to the
point that Brünnhilde has disappeared from his memory
and he has fallen in love with Gutrune. He drinks blood
brotherhood with Gunther. Gunther: "I will gladly give you
Gutrune." Siegfried: "I will bring Brünnhilde to you."

With the help of the Tarnhelm, he approaches Brünnhilde,
pretending to be Gunther. He takes the Ring away from
Brünnhilde, and when she realizes that she has been betrayed, she reveals Siegfried's secret to Hagen, that When
he bathed in the blood of the dead Fafner and thus became invulnerable, a leaf had fallen from a branch onto

that spot, and he remains unprotected there. Now Hagen wounds Siegfried with a spear and later says that this was caused by a hunting accident [Jewish cowardice].

On his deathbed, Siegfried again remembers Brünnhilde. She has a funeral pyre built and Siegfried's body placed on it. She follows her beloved into the flames. The curse of the Ring [that which is terrible about Jewish, capitalistic world domination] has been made ineffective through the noble race and its great ability to love. [Wagner's vision is parallel to Hitler's image of a new world order of "pure blood."] Valhalla burns. [The Thousand-Year Reich perishes.]

Valhalla burns

Curtain

6.7. *Parsifal*

The legendary Third Reich Nazi Ordensburg Vogelsang in the northern Eifel region is considered to be the second largest National Socialist building in Germany, following only the Parteitag buildings in Nuremberg. Training at Vogelsang was designed to educate the Aryan members of the "master race" in the "spirit of the fight for Adolf Hitler." Beginning on May 1, 1936, approximately 500 "nobles" were given military and ideological training to make them into "torchbearers of the nation." Several castles (here Vogelsang) were to serve as a "symbol of the greatness and dignity of the National Socialist worldview" on a daily basis to those that were to be trained as National Socialist leaders, according to Reichsarbeitsführer Robert Ley, one of the "educational theorists" of National Socialism. He combined racism, mass murder and war apocalypse to shape a "great and dignified" pseudo religious ideology.[14]

An opera performance is fitting here as a cultural and educational component in line with the pseudo-religious and mythological concept of the NSDAP. In his "Bühnenweihfestspiel Parsifal" (sacred festival drama), Wagner reveals both worlds – the demon of criminal Jewish world domination, which is overcome by the Aryan heroic figure Parsifal and is represented with the help of a Germanic-Christian liturgy.

Characters:

- Amfortas, King of the Holy Grail
- Titurel, his father
- Gurnemanz, head trainer of the Nazi Knights of the Grail
- Parsifal, the Germanic-German heroic figure
- Klingsor, representative of the Jewish demon
- Kundry, Jewess dependent on Klingsor
- Two Grail knights
- Four squires
- Klingsor's flower maidens

---

[14] Peter Prestel and Rudolf Sporrer, Film "Hitlers Ordensburgen" (3sat, August 28, 2009).

- A voice from above
- Chorus, the brotherhood of the Grail Knights
- Women's chorus, boys' voices from above

Time and place: 1937, Nazi Ordensburg Vogelsang

Nazi Ordensburg Vogelsang Castle

ACT I

Amfortas, the King of the Vogelsang Castle of the Holy Grail, has a painful wound in the side of his body in the same place as that of the crucified Lord and that cannot heal. The magician Klingsor, who represents the dark, un-Christian power, had wounded Amfortas with the "holy spear" and then taken this magic weapon away from him. Without this spear, the wound of the ailing King of the Grail cannot heal even now.

Before Amfortas is carried in to the Meeting Hall on a litter for his bath, Kundry appears. Wagner's stage directions tell us: "Kundry rushes in, almost staggering. Wild clothing, her skirts tucked up; long snakeskin belt hanging down; disheveled, black hair in loose braids; deep ruddy-brown complexion; piercing black eyes, sometimes flashing wildly, often fixed and lifeless." [At the beginning of this sacred festival drama, Wagner already characterizes Kundry through her appearance by observing her Jewish, foreign nature, as also elucidated in other writings of his and then later further carried forth as far as Hitler.] The two squires regard her as an enemy of the Order.

"If the balsam doesn't help Amfortas," says Kundry, "then Arabia has nothing more to heal him. Ask no more! I am weary!" Amfortas is now carried in, lying on his litter, and asks for Gawain, one of the Knights of the Grail. He is not present, however, and is thus violating the Grail's commandments. Amfortas fears: "Oh, woe to him if he falls into Klingsor's clutches!" Klingsor is the embodiment of the demonic power of the Jews. Gurnemanz tells the squires about this later. Amfortas now relates his vision: "I

Feldherrnhalle (Field Marshall's Hall)

await the one intended for me: wise through compassion; an innocent fool. I think I will recognize him. I might call him Death!" Gurnemanz, the head trainer of the Nazi leadership school, hands Amfortas a vessel with balsam that has been given to him by Kundry. Amfortas asks where it comes from and learns that it is from the sinner Kundry, who has brought it from a distant place. He wants to thank her, but she refuses. The litter with the ailing Grail King is carried toward the bath.

In Wagner's prose drafts of "Jesus of Nazareth," this sinner is named Mary Magdalene. She is forgiven because of her ability to feel compassion for Jesus. According to Wagner's ideology of the downfall of the Jews, this would obviously not be possible, because it denies them the ability to experience compassion.

In another draft, Wagner's Buddhist drama entitled "The Victors," Prakriti from the lowest caste is in love – against the rules – with Ananda from the highest caste. Prakriti approaches Buddha to ask him for help. He asks her whether she would be willing to satisfy the conditions for permission to be able to and to be permitted to love Ananda. Prakriti speaks of her wish for an erotic relationship with Ananda and is dismayed when she learns that she must respect and share his oath of chastity. She has no choice but to experience the torture of a hopeless love, at the same time to renounce it, and thus to be accepted in the community of Buddha through complete redemption[15].

Richard Wagner himself only names one such person, the Jewish author Ludwig Börne (1786-1837), in "Jewishness in Music" and describes his painful and successful "rebirth." [16] Wagner's religion of the future becomes even clearer in a draft piece of prose on Parsifal and in his description of the role of Kundry: "Kundry lives a boundless life with constantly changing rebirths, resulting from an ancient curse similar to that of the eternal Jew that damns her to spread the suffering of seduction among men in new guises. Foretold for her are redemption, dissolution, and total death."

Two squires say to Kundry and everyone present: "With her magic potion [balm], she will be the complete ruin of

---

[15] Karl Heckel, "Jesus von Nazareth – Buddha ('Die Sieger') – Parsifal," *Bayreuther Blätter*, 1891).
[16] Richard Wagner, *Sämtliche Schriften, Vol. 5* (CD-Rom).

our Master [Amfortas]. She hates us. Just see the malicious look [she] is giving us. She is a heathen, a sorceress." Gurnemanz explains: "Perhaps she is living to again atone for some guilt from an earlier life that was not forgiven then."

A squire: "So it may be, her guilt that has brought such distress on us." Gurnemanz says that Titurel found her already "sleeping, as if dead" here in the woods, at the time he was building the castle [Vogelsang]. Gurnemanz now finds Kundry again "shortly after the misfortune struck, that that evildoer [Klingsor, the Jewish demon] brought upon us so shamefully beyond the mountains." And, turning to Kundry, he says: "Where were you when Amfortas lost the holy spear? Why did you not help then?" The telling answer of the Jewess [according to Wagner and Hitler] is: "I never help!"

This is the curse that points out the path toward salvation. "Helping through compassion!" Kundry struggles against this deliverance from Judaism through her own strength, which leads her repeatedly to rebirths as a Jewess.

An initial ink to this assessment is found in the often quoted sentence written by Wagner: "To become a man together with us means, first of all, for the Jew essentially to cease being a Jew." [17] Later, in Act II, Kundry permits herself to be used again by the magician Klingsor, as a representative of demonic Jewry, and thus remains a Jewess as viewed by Wagner and National Socialism.

Gurnemanz now tells the story of the Holy Grail and how the then protected Amfortas became weak in the arms of a "terribly beautiful woman." The dark force, the devilish [Jewish] demon in the form of the magician Klingsor, had committed "the beautiful woman," Kundry, to deliver Amfortas to Klingsor. "In her arms he [Amfortas] lay drunk-

---

[17] Ibid.

en." The latter wrested the holy spear away from him and inflicted upon him the wound in his side that "will never heal." The father of the current Grail king, Titurel, had once received the holy spear and Grail from the hand of the "Savior's angel messengers," so that he could defend himself against the "cunning and might of savage foes" who "threatened the realm of pure faith." [A clear reference to the hostile world Jewry and the pure Aryan race in the Nazi ideology.] Titurel than built the present sanctuary for the spear and the Grail, represented by the Nazi Ordensburg Vogelsang. Klingsor, he continued, wished to atone, but was not willing to "stifle" his sinful life. Full of hate, he became a demonic magician.

"Wise through compassion, the innocent fool," a naive young man, so to speak. It is said that he can free Amfortas from his suffering. [Here, too, a nod from the basically uneducated Adolf Hitler, who didn't think much of the educated elite among the Nazis.]

The "innocent fool" has shot a swan in the woods and is brought with the dying animal to Gurnemanz and the Grail knights. Gurnemanz asks him whether he has done this and reproaches him for it: "An outrageous act! How could you commit murder, here in the holy forest? What did that good swan do to you? Speak, boy. Do you recognize your great guilt? How could you commit this deed?" And the naïve Parsifal answers: "I did not know." Now Gurnemanz wants to know where the young man comes from, who he is, who his father is. Parsifal knows nothing, not even his own name.

Head trainer Gurnemanz now sends his fellow members of the Nazi order away. They should not neglect Amfortas

in the bath. He remains alone with Kundry and Parsifal.
Gurnemanz keeps questioning the young man. He thinks
he is a noble and learns that his mother's name is Her-
zeleide [Brokenheart], who – according to Kundry – "hid
the fatherless child in the woods after the heroic death of
her spouse Gamuret," to rear him there "a stranger to
weapons." But Parsifal tells them how he made a bow and
arrow himself, and Kundry explains that he attacked
"thieves and giants" and they all learned to fear him.
Kundry reports that his mother is dead, and Parsifal "seiz-
es her by the throat." Gurnemanz separates them. [Wag-
ner's stage direction: Parsifal begins to tremble violently.]
Parsifal says "I feel faint," and Kundry brings water for
him to drink. Gurnemanz praises her for this. But Kundry
recognizes her Jewish fate, which can only end with her
"demise." "I never do good. I long only for rest. Only rest!
Sleep, sleep! Oh, that no one would wake me! No! Not
sleep! Terror grips me! The time has come. Sleep, I must
sleep." [Repeated references to Wagner's statements regarding the "Demise of the Jews," such as in "Jewishness
in Music" up to Hitler's extermination mania.]

Amfortas is carried back from the bath and asked by Titurel, his father, to recite the liturgy with the Holy Grail.
Amfortas should open the vessel and remove the chalice.
"In this service, you may atone for your sins," orders Titurel. "Uncover the Grail!" Amfortas refuses to do this at
first and bemoans the incomparable torment the sight of
the Grail causes him: "What is the wound, the agony to be
condemned to serve this office. Woeful inheritance. Oh,
unparalleled punishment" Then he does open the Grail's
vessel. "The ebb of my own sinful blood; in a frenzied
flight, it must flow back to me, to pour itself into the

world of sinful passion with wild awe. Once again, it breaks open the gate and streams through it, here through the wound, similar to his, inflicted by a blow from the same spear. The hot, sinful blood, ever renewed from the spring of desire, ah! that no repentance of mine can ever still! Mercy! Mercy! All-merciful one! Take back my inheritance, heal the wound, so that I may die holy and pure for you!" Wagner's direction: Amfortas becomes unconscious, and then regains consciousness. Boys uncover the Grail. Voices sing from above: "Take my body, take my blood, for the sake of our love. Take my blood, take my body, in remembrance of me!" It is becoming dark. A ray of light falls from above on the crystal Grail. Titurel can be heard: "O holy bliss, how brightly our Lord greets us today." Amfortas has lifted the vessel and blessed the people around him with it. The boys enclose it again in its shrine. It is becoming light again, and the knights of the Grail celebrate their meal with bread and wine.

Opening the Grail

The proximity of the Bühnenweihfestspiel (sacred festival drama) to the National Socialist mystique is demonstrated by the chorus of knights together with the voices from above: "Take of the bread, change it boldly into bodily strength and power, faithful until death, steadfast in every effort to do the Savior's works! Take of the wine, turn it anew into the fiery blood of life, joyfully united, to fight as brothers blessed with holy courage."

For comparison, here is an excerpt from the speech of Joseph Goebbels at the Berlin Sport Palace on February 18, 1943: "We Germans are armed against weakness and vulnerability. The blows and accidents of war only give us additional strength, fierce determination, and a psychological and combative activity that prepares us to meet all difficulties and hindrances with revolutionary vigor."

In a kind of Christian-Germanic liturgy, the Nazi Grail knights are thus committed to fight the enemy, the demon of Jewish world domination. The participants of this fascist round table and Amfortas leave the stage. Gurnemanz turns to Parsifal, who has silently followed this ceremony with great attention and throws him out of the Nazi Ordensburg. "Off with you. But Gurnemanz has advice for you: In the future, leave the swans here in peace; the gander should look for a goose!"

ACT II

Inside a brothel in a red-light district controlled by Jews

Klingsor, the boss of this under- or anti-world speaks: "The time has come. The fool [Parsifal] is already being drawn to my magic castle. In a deathlike sleep, she [Kundry] is held fast by the curse. Up then! Get to work!" Wagner's staging directions speak of "mysterious gestures toward the abyss, darkness in the depths, magic instruments. Klingsor calls Kundry: "Arise! To me! Your master calls you, nameless one, primeval she-devil, rose of hell! You were Herodias. Kundry, here! Come here! Are you awake? You have fallen under my spell again today at the right time." "Sleep, deep sleep, death!" She wants to "cease to exist." Klingsor now reminds her that it is her duty today to seduce Parsifal, who is protected by his naiveté. "If he sinks into your arms, he will be felled by the [holy] spear," namely the one that already lastingly wounded Amfortas.

Parsifal fights his way successfully through to Klingsor's brothel. Change in scene. According to Richard Wagner's idea, there is a tropical flower garden, with beautiful young girls, only lightly dressed. Seduction! As imagined today, this would be a kind of luxurious brothel with a bathing landscape and a massage salon. Cacophony of the voices of women who are searching for their lovers or clients now killed by Parsifal. "Who is our enemy? There he stands. Why did you strike down our lovers?"

Change in scene. The young women and the naïve Parsifal come closer. The girls offer themselves to him: "We don't play for money. We play for love's favors [sex]. Come, pretty boy! Let me kiss your lips! Don't you dare?"

Parsifal: "Stop it. You won't catch me!" Kundry calls him by his name and sends the girls away. She gains his confidence by speaking about his past, his mother, the pain of leaving her, her death. Parsifal is terribly sad and overwhelmed. Feelings of compassion arise in him that Wagner claims Jews do not have. [Wagner's stage direction: Kundry bends over Parsifal's face in a reclining position and places her arm around him: "Learn to know love." She has bent her head completely over his and plants her lips on his mouth for a long kiss.]

Now Parsifal suddenly jumps up with a gesture of utmost terror, and his demeanor expresses a terrible change. "Amfortas! The wound! Fearful sorrow. I saw the wound bleeding, now it bleeds in me." Parsifal remembers the liturgy and Amfortas's suffering when the Grail vessel was opened. Kundry: "Promised hero! Flee this madness!" [Come to me.] Parsifal now recognizes in Kundry the [Jewish] sin to which Amfortas has already fallen victim: "Corruptress! Get away from me! Away forever!" Kundry speaks of the curse that keeps taking her through new lives and does not bring her salvation. [This also shows Wagner's characterization of the Jewess.]

Parsifal: "You would be damned with me if I should forget my mission for an hour embraced in your arms. Salvation [shall] never be granted to you. I also offer redemption to you, sinner." But Kundry insists: "Let me love you, godly one. Then, too, you would grant me redemption. Be mine for just one hour!" Parsifal rejects her: "Away, wretched woman!"

Kundry now curses Parsifal, and Klingsor appears. He hurls the holy spear toward Parsifal, but the weapon remains hovering above the head of the young man. Parsifal grabs the spear and makes the sign of the cross with it in the direction of the demon: "With this sign, I destroy your magic. As it heals the wound you gave him [Amfortas] with it, may it destroy the fraudulent splendor!" The brothel disappears. [The Jewish immorality, the Jewish demon have been conquered.]

ACT III

In the meantime, Gurnemanz has grown old and is now an aged hermit. The activities in the Nazi castle have fallen into a deep sleep. Gurnemanz hears groaning and discovers Kundry: "You crazy woman! Don't you have anything to say to me? Is this how you thank me for waking you once more from your deathlike sleep?" Kundry can only manage to speak roughly and brokenly: "Serve, serve." She fetches a pitcher with water. Parsifal appears in a full suit of armor and carrying the holy spear. Gurnemanz to him: "Do you offer no greeting to me? Even if your vows constrain you to silence, you are in a hallowed place. One does not come here armed, with a closed visor, shield and spear. Don't you know that today is the most holy Good Friday?"

Parsifal puts aside his armor and the spear. Gurnemanz finally recognizes him again, and Kundry confirms his identity. Parsifal to Gurnemanz: "I rejoice at finding you again!" He had wanted to go to Amfortas, to bring him salvation. The knights, answers Gurnemanz, are desperately awaiting comfort, salvation, as Amfortas has refused for so long to uncover the Grail: "The Grail has remained enclosed within the shrine for a long time. Thus its guardian [Amfortas], repenting of his sin, since he cannot die when he beholds it, hopes to hasten his death, and to end his torment with his life. The divine nourishment is now denied us. Therefore our heroes' strength is exhausted." Parsifal: "And it was I, I who caused all this misery?" Kundry now brings water from the holy spring.

For the death rites of his father, Titurel, Amfortas is now to serve the "long-neglected office" and the liturgy with the Grail. Kundry and Gurnemanz cleanse Parsifal of the dust from his long trip and anoint his feet and head. Gurnemanz speaks of the fulfillment of the promise and greets Parsifal as the new king, a leader of the Nazi Vogelsang Castle. Parsifal sprinkles Kundry with the holy water and blesses her with it. She weeps bitterly during this. "Noon." sings Gurnemanz, "The hour has come. Permit your servant to guide you, my lord!"

Entrance of the knights

Scene change back to the Meeting Hall in the Castle. As in Act I, the knights enter. This time, it is a funeral march. The procession includes the covered shrine with the Grail and Titurel's open casket. Amfortas is carried in on the litter.

The chorus of knights commands him "to do his duty" and to show the Grail. But he would rather die and therefore refuses. The knights: "You must, you must!" He asks them to kill him: "Draw your weapons! Thrust your swords deep, deep up to the hilt! Get up, you heroes! Kill the sinner with his torment! Then the Grail will shine for you of itself!"

Parsifal enters, interrupts the occurrences, and touches Amfortas's wound with the holy spear. He thus absolves him, so that the wound can heal: "Blessed be your suffering, that gave compassion's highest power and the might of purest wisdom to the timid fool! The holy spear, I bring it back to you." He now uncovers the Grail and thereby returns to the brotherhood of knights the strength they had lacked for so long. Kundry sinks to the earth, lifeless. Kundry is the eternal Jewess in Wagner's final work. She had laughed at Christ when he was nailed to the cross. Since then she has undergone transmigration, wandering through time and space. After a good four and a half hours of wandering through all the keys related to A flat major, she is again baptized by the new Grail king [Parsifal] and dies with a modulation into the simplest A minor. This constitutes one of the central instances demonstrating the thesis that Wagner's antisemitism can indeed be heard in his music."[18]

Curtain

[18] Eleonore Brüning, "Neues vom Giftmischer," *Frankfurter Allgemeine Zeitung*, April 7, 2013.

6.8. Rienzi

The story is no longer set in Rome, but at the Bayreuth Festspielhaus. Freedom of expression makes an additional alienation possible, that of turning the Führer's command post, the "Wolfsschanze," into the Bayreuth Festspielhaus. Seen as the set therefore is the Festspielhaus, rather than the Führer's Headquarters, the barracks in which Count Claus Schenk von Stauffenberg attempted to assassinate Hitler on July 20, 1944.

Stauffenberg's co-conspirators consist of present-day authors, critics, journalists, artists, and subsidizing foundations. They appear in the last scene as the chorus.

The main role, the usurper Rienzi, becomes Hitler, the last great Führer. Irene becomes Eva Braun.

Great tragic opera in 5 acts by Richard Wagner

Time and place: Adolf Hitler's command post, now the Festspielhaus in Bayreuth

A stage concept, described here briefly – and only the fourth scene [finale]

Chorus of present-day media, authors, artists and foundations: Come here – hurry to us – bring stones – bring firebrand – he is cursed, he has been banned. May perdition fall on him [Hitler, naturally] – and death! [Hitler appears with Eva Braun on the balcony of the Festspielhaus.]

Hitler: "Do you still know me? The Führer needs quiet, you degenerate ones! Say, is this how you Germans show your pride?"

Chorus: "Get going! Stone him!"

Hitler: "Bear in mind, who made you great and free? Do you not remember the exultation with which you greeted me back then, when I gave you freedom and peace? For your own sake, I beg of you: Think of your German vow."

Chorus: "Don't listen to him – set the Festspielhaus on fire."

Hitler: "You wretches! Do you think you can destroy me? The greatest Führer curses you! May this house be cursed and burnt and rot and wither away completely! You shall see the Führer return!"

The Festspielhaus built onstage is set on fire on several sides by the stagehands. Now it is completely on fire. One can see Hitler and Eva Braun on the balcony. They are holding each other and are surrounded by flames. The conspirators are throwing stones at them.

The upper part of the Festspielhaus, the balcony on which the two of them are standing, finally collapses with a loud noise. Hitler's end is like that of Rienzi, the Führer's favorite hero.

The end of the Bayreuth Festival Hall

Curtain

Part VII

Wagner in Israel

The average person one might encounter thinks of the composer Richard Wagner as someone who has written very loud music and whose works last much too long, according to music critic Alex Ross. We who interpret Wagner on the stage can confirm this impression often enough. But one should not forget, according to Mr. Ross, that Richard Wagner's music dramas also had a strong influence on Baudelaire, Mallarmé, Proust, Joyce, Mann, Cather, Kandinsky, Isadora Duncan, Eisenstein, and many others. For several decades, however, productions of Wagner's music have been unofficially banned in Israel.

This taboo dates back to 1938, to the murderous Night of Broken Glass in Nazi Germany, when a member of what was then the Palestine Symphony Orchestra asked the conductor, Arturo Toscanini (1867-1957), to remove the Overture of *Die Meistersinger von Nürnberg* from the program. Toscanini, who was an avowed opponent of Hitler, saw no connection between Wagner's music and National Socialism, but still fulfilled the orchestra's request. On the other hand, he conducted many Wagner concerts in the USA during the Second World War.[1]

It should be remembered, however, that he cancelled his planned appearance in 1936 at the Bayreuth Festival and,

---

[1] Alex Ross, "The Case for Wagner in Israel," Culture Desk, *The New Yorker* (Sept. 25, 2012).

as a protest against the Nazis, conducted *Die Meistersinger von Nürnberg* at the Salzburg Festival instead. In 1898, Toscanini had also opened the season at La Scala in Milan with the *Meistersinger*.[2]

In recent decades, conductors have repeatedly made efforts to perform Wagner in Israel. In 1981, for example, Zubin Mehta offered the "Liebestod" from *Tristan und Isolde* as an encore at a concert, but gave opponents of the composer an opportunity to leave the concert hall beforehand. Protested by some members of the audience, Daniel Barenboim also conducted the Overture to *Tristan und Isolde* in 2001 in Jerusalem. Furthermore, in 2012, to mark Richard Wagner's 200th birthday, the Israel Wagner Society again attempted to arrange a Wagner concert, this time at Tel Aviv University. This performance was finally cancelled, and the intended substitute date at the Hilton Hotel was also called off.

The main argument that was given against performing Wagner was that this could cause traumatic memories to surface among the survivors of the Holocaust. It was common knowledge, of course, that the Nazis played music by Richard Wagner on every possible occasion. Efforts in Israel to verify this fact, however, revealed that Wagner was played less often at the concentration camps than Wagner opponents would like to believe. To the contrary, survivors say that it was Johann Strauss waltzes, Suppé overtures, operettas or military marches that blasted out of all of the loudspeakers. Auschwitz survivor Zofia Posmysz

---

[2] Bernd Weikl/Peter Bendixen, *Freispruch für Richard Wagner?* (Leipzig, 2012).

says that she turns off her radio when music by Johann Strauss is played, as she finds it unbearable.

Interestingly enough, as Alex Ross describes it, Theodor Herzl (1860-1904) related the following about the very period during which he was writing his famous book – *The Jewish State*: "My only relaxation came from Richard Wagner's music, which I enjoyed in the evening, particularly *Tannhäuser,* an opera I listened to as often as possible."[3]

Many members of the younger generation of Israelis have been able to distance themselves from their grandparents' negative feelings toward Wagner. One young musicologist approached this topic intellectually and came to a different conclusion.

Irad Atir completed his MA in musicology at Tel Aviv University and then his PhD at Bar-Ilan University in June 2012 with a dissertation entitled "Judaism and Germanism in Richard Wagner's Art" that won an award from Yad Vashem's International Institute for Holocaust Studies. His interview with journalist Haggai Hiltron was published in the Israeli newspaper *Ha'aretz* on January 28, 2013. Atir's answers during the interview included the following conclusions:

"Wagner was not the antisemite people believe he was. His criticism of Jews was part of his opposition to the general sociopolitical and cultural situation in the 19th century – including that of the non-Jewish society of this era. Wagner criticized certain aspects of the Germans as well, such as their conservatism, unconditional religiosity, pride in the aristocracy, and militarism. On the other hand, he targeted

---

[3] Alex Ross, "The Case for Wagner in Israel."

Jewish separatism. Generally speaking, our composer felt that there were good and bad Germans – and good and bad Jews."

Furthermore, Felix Mendelssohn's music had a strong influence on Wagner, and he frequently copied the Jewish composer. Irad Atir provides examples to prove his point. In his Overture to *Das Rheingold,* for example, the maestro drew from Mendelssohn's *Die schöne Melusine.* Other examples are the "Todesverkündigung" in *Die Walküre.* It uses parts of Mendelssohn's *Scottish Symphony.* The "Ride of the Valkyries" has similarities with Mendelssohn's *Fingal's Cave* and was written in the same key. The motif of the "Holy Grail" in *Parsifal* stems from Mendelssohn's *Reformation Symphony,* and the musical motif for Freia in the *Ring of the Nibelung* is the musical theme of the "Wedding March" in *A Midsummer Night's* Dream by Mendelssohn.

"Wagner", says Atir, "knew more about Jews and Judaism and worked more with Jews than all the other composers of his time. His bias against individuals and groups was complex and could change at any time. Even his dire essay "Jewishness in Music" ends with an appeal to unite the Jewish and German cultures." The feelings Israelis have toward Richard Wagner are also based on faulty information, according to Atir. "When Israelis insist that Wagner was a Nazi, they ought to remember that the composer died 6 years before Hitler was even born. Hopefully, newer information will be able to change these negative feelings in Israel"[4].

---

[4] Haggai Hiltron, *Ha'aretz,* January 28, 2013.

The German media did not report on Irad Atir's positive view of Richard Wagner and his statements and works. And the young Israeli would presumably not have been able to earn his degree at a German university with this doctoral thesis. Wagner's antisemitism and his "collaboration" with Hitler are part of the curriculum in many degree programs in theater arts here. This is in part based on the premise that staging concepts of Wagner's works that do not reflect this are likely to remain unsuccessful, given the current trend, and would thus be detrimental to both the career of the graduate implementing such concepts – assuming they are accepted for production by a theater at all – and to the reputation of the institution granting this doctorate.

Judging from Irad Atir's statements, it is possible that Wagner will soon be seen on the opera stage in Israel. At the same time, unfortunately, efforts continue to be made in Germany to morph his music dramas into a form that is so misleading that it deserves to be banned.

Epilogue

A survivor of the Holocaust, Roman Kent, would add an Eleventh Commandment if he could: "You should never be a bystander." And the German President, Joachim Gauck, could never comprehend the fact that horrendous crimes like those of the Nazis could be committed in the context of the honorable German culture.

I support Roman Kent and will never permit myself to be a bystander. In view of the facts I have described in this book, I therefore feel that I must publicly cast doubt on what the German President referred to as an honorable cultural nation – Germany – in the present time as well. I must also ask whether this highly respected representative of our nation does not see, or does not learn or read, what is happening in our theaters and how this honorable culture is being reprehensibly destroyed.

While swastikas were worn and Jews were shot or gassed in *Tannhäuser* at the opera house in Dusseldorf, while blood flowed everywhere, this has happened and is happening in straight plays in Germany as well. One such example occurred in Munich on May 26, 2015. Alexander Altmann of the *Münchner Merkur* reported:

"Sensitive theatergoers should not subject themselves to this evening. But even less sensitive individuals may also stagger out of the Munich Marstall (Residenztheater) after they have seen Oliver Frljić's stage performance *Balkan macht frei,* whose title already alludes to the perverted slogan 'Arbeit macht frei' (Work will free you) seen above the concentration camp gates. At the premiere, members of the audience fled, protested, and screamed 'Stop!' What had happened?

"You see three actors with cardboard signs hanging around their necks. On them are names like Johann Wolfgang von Goethe, Brecht and Handke, as well as Castorf and Kušej. A fourth actor, Franz Pätzold, plays a Bosnian stage director named Oliver Frljić, a wild man from the Balkans, who guns down the five icons of Central European culture on these cardboard signs – in effigy, one could say. Amen.

"In the following scene, Pätzold verbally abuses the audience. While this is happening, it would be best not to sit in the first few rows, as Pätzold's Frljić directly addresses the members of the audience who are sitting there. 'You are gawkers,' he rails at them in a terrifying rage. The reference here is the decadence cliché of the rich, mollycoddled Westerners, who do not demonstrate the proper 'bearing.' The SS men who drove the Jews into the gas chambers, to the contrary, did have the proper 'bearing.' Then he curses today's Germans, calling them bio-fascists, and screams that the Jews ought to be gassed. This is followed by a waterboarding scene that was so unbearable that some feisty women in the audience stormed onto the stage to end the scene."[1] This happened in Munich.

And in Berlin: "Bloody, sadomasochistic sex on the stage: Does that still shock us? Blood, semen, shit, urine. A normal evening at the theater on May 27, 2015, at the Berlin Volksbühne. The premiere of *The 120 Days of Sodom*. The

---

[1] Alexander Altmann, "Eklat am Resi: Zuschauer stürmen auf die Bühne," *Münchner Merkur*, May 26, 2015.

stage director is Johann Kresnik (75). "The elite of the Berlin cultural world is delighted. They get to see perversion, pain, desperation. The play is based on a legendary cinematic orgy of violence. At that time (1975), it was the greatest scandal in the history of the cinema. The director, Pier Paolo Pasolini, died at the age of 53 and did not live to see the premiere. The film had been banned. When it was later shown in movie theaters, Pasolini was dead. He had been murdered by a young male prostitute in Ostia, an Italian seaside resort.

"Is this play, which is now being performed in Berlin, a scandal? No, but all efforts are being made to make it one. The problem is that the audience has become accustomed to calculated provocations. There is hardly a contemporary play these days without nudity. So how can this be taken a step further? In *Sodom,* the actors urinate on one another. But these days, this doesn't stop anyone from enjoying a canapé with smoked salmon during the intermission." [2]

"The penis is cut off the man on the cross, then to be eaten with great relish, along with the bishop's feces. Torn out intestines are also served. There is plenty of blood, and urine and semen and ongoing copulation are on the menu. A baby is cut out of the body of a pregnant woman who is still alive, then to be chopped up and grilled. As a questionable climax at the Volksbühne — as is also the case in the production of *Balkan macht frei* at the Munich Residenztheater that is currently being hotly disputed — the

---

[2] Alexander von Schönburg, "Blutiger Sadomaso-Sex auf der Bühne," *Bild,* May 28, 2015.

practice of torture through waterboarding is demonstrated as well…

"Ismael Ivo, formerly the icon of modern dance in Berlin, puts himself totally at the disposal of this jolting theater as co-choreographer and occasional dancer. Nothing remains of the finely wrought work that was once so venerated. And Gottfried Helnwein, famed for his hyperrealistic pictures of wounded children, has wrapped the entire ensemble in bloody bandages. He has dead children rain down from the flyloft and has the entire matter play out in a gigantic store. Coca-Colas stand next to BP in the overcrowded shelves, drones next to Burger King, and so forth. The consumption-oriented kids take what they want, until they are mowed down by machine gun salvos. And they do it again. The killer argument is: 'History is dead!' "[3]

Any free art is permitted to put provocations like this on the market, as long as it does not violate the rules that have been legislated (sexual harassment). But these free artists have to find their own customers. Examples of this are performances in the movie houses or the erotic theaters on the so-called "sinners' mile" in Hamburg's St. Pauli district. There the desires of a voyeuristic audience can be satisfied, but they have to pay for their own tickets.

As much as 80 percent of the financial needs of the state or municipal theaters in Germany, however, are subsidized by the general public through a kind of "mandatory contribution." This is the reason that these theaters ought to fulfill the state educational mandate, which does not apply

---

[3] Ute Büsing, "Die 120 Tage von Sodom an der Berliner Volksbühne," *RBB Kultur*, May 28, 2015.

to free art. To the contrary, for example, the Metropolitan Opera in New York is financed by private donors – who would never agree to performances like those seen in Dusseldorf, Munich or Berlin.

More about the status quo: Especially in Germany, a constantly growing discrepancy exists between the music and the singers, on the one hand, and the stage on the other. While singers aim toward building a loving relationship with their audience, stage directors and set designers are conducting a private war against their customers in the auditorium, whom they seem to loathe. And all of this is financed with tax money.

This is why I truly hope that this book will be understood as an appeal to all of its readers, no matter where they may be, not to be bystanders either. There is no need to forbid the performance of Richard Wagner's works anywhere. He had nothing to do with the Holocaust. Rather, he and his works were abused by the Nazis for their own purposes, and this abuse is still being continued today in brutal fashion. Those responsible for their criminal actions today, for the destruction of our culture, must be called to account. A society without culture led to the crimes of the Nazis back then. In the 21st century, the state educational mandate was designed to prevent this from happening in theaters in Germany. Unfortunately – as witnessed by the examples above – it is not being adhered to.

Bernd Weikl

Glossary

BDM (Bund Deutscher Mädel)	League of German Girls. The girls' wing of the Nazi youth movement, parallel to the Hitlerjugend (Hitler Youth) for boys
Berghof	Adolf Hitler's home in the Obersalzberg region of the Bavarian Alps near Berchtesgaden
Berliner Sportpalast	Berlin Sports Palace. A multipurpose winter sports venue and meeting hall in the Schöneberg section of Berlin
Blutschande	Racial pollution. Sexual relations between Aryans and non-Aryans, punishable by law
Bühnenweihfestspiel	Sacred festival drama. Wagner's description of *Parsifal*
Bund Reichskriegsflagge	Imperial War Flag Society. A paramilitary organization founded by Ernst Röhm in 1923
Deutscher Kampfbund	German Combat League. A union of patriotic fighting societies and the German National Socialist party founded in the 1920s

Deutschlandlied	German national anthem ("Deutschland, Deutschland über alles")
Festspielhaus	Festival Theater in Bayreuth
Festwiese	Fairground or festival grounds
Fremdengesetzgebung	Aliens Law
Führerpalast	Führer's Palace
Gauleiter	Head of a Gau (regional district)
Gemerk	Marker's box
Generalfeldmarschall	General Field Marshall
Generalgouvernement	General Government. The part of Poland administered by Germany during WWII
Grosse Halle	Great Hall
Gruft	Vault
Gruppenführer	Group leader or section commander. Highest SA and SS ranking, equivalent to (US/UK) Major General
Heil	Common greeting during Third Reich (Hail!)
Obergruppenführersaal	SS Generals' Hall
Ordensburg	NSDAP training school in a fortress built in the Middle Ages
Parteitag	NSDAP party (rally) days

Rassenschande	Racial shame (see Blutschande)
Reichsarbeitsführer	Reich Labor Leader
Reichsführer SS	Title held by Heinrich Himmler, head of the SS. Equal on paper to the rank of Generalfeldmarschall, but in fact more akin to Reichs-marschall from 1942 onward, as Himmler amassed ever greater power
Reichshaus der SS-Gruppen-führer	Addition to the Wewelsburg castle for the SS-Gruppen-führer
Reichskulturkammer	Reich Chamber of Culture
Reichsleiter	National leader or Reich lead-er, the second highest political rank of the NSDAP, next on-ly to the office of the Führer
Reichsmarschall	Marshal of the Reich, the highest rank in the German armed forces during World War II (held only by Her-mann Göring)
Reichsministerium	Reich Ministry
Reichsparteitag	State Party Days, referred to in English as the Nuremberg Rallies. Nazi party rallies, held annually in Nuremberg near the date of the Autumn equi-nox before the outbreak of war in 1939

Reichsparteitagsgelände	Nazi party rally grounds
Reichspogromnacht	Known as the "Night of Broken Glass," November 9–10, 1938, when mob violence against Jews broke out all over Germany
Reichswehr	National Defense (armed forces) of the Weimar Republic, renamed the Wehrmacht in 1935, comprised of the Army and Navy
Reichssportfeld	Sports complex built in Berlin for the Olympic Games of 1936
Reichstag	Reich Parliament
Rüstungsminister	Minister of Armaments
Schutzstaffel	Protection Squadron, known as the SS
Tarnhelm	Magic helmet
Waffen SS	Armed SS. The combat branch of the Schutzstaffel
Werktreue	Remaining faithful to the original work
Wewelsburg	A castle near Büren, Westphalia, taken over and restored by Heinrich Himmler as an SS officers' training school and cult center

Wolfsschanze	Wolf's Lair. Hitler's first World War II Eastern Front military headquarters, where he spent much of his time during the war following the launch of Operation Barbarossa.

Bibliography

Adolf Hitler. *Bilder aus dem Leben des Führers.* (Altona/Bahrenfeld: Bilderdienst Alias, 1936).

Adorno, Theodor W. "Versuch über Wagner." *Die musikalischen Monographien* (Berlin: Verlag Suhrkamp, 1952).

Altman, Alexander. "Eklat am Resi: Zuschauer stürmen auf die Bühne." *Münchner Merkur,* May 26, 2015.

Augstein, Rudolf. "Siegfried, Lohengrin, Parsifal - Hitler?" *Der Spiegel,* July 21, 1997.

Bärsch, Claus Ekkehard. *Der junge Goebbels, Erlösung und Vernichtung.* (Munich: Verlag Wilhelm Fink, 2004).

Barth, Christian T. *Goebbels und die Juden.* (Paderborn: Verlag Schönigh, 2003).

Bayreuther Festspielführer (Bayreuth, 1936).

Bein, Alex. *Die Judenfrage: Biographie eines Weltproblems.* (Munich: Deutscher Verlags-Anstalt, 1980).

Bendixen, Peter and Bernd Weikl. *Einführung in die Kultur- und Kunstökonomie,* 3rd Ed. (Wiesbaden: VS Verlag für Sozialwissenschaften, 2011).

Brecht, Bertold. *Der aufhaltsame Aufstieg der Arturo Ui.* (Berlin: Suhrkamp, 1973).

Beyer, Barbara. *Warum Oper?* (Berlin: Alexander Verlag, 2005).

Boberski, Heiner. *Das Engelwerk. Theorie und Praxis des Opus Angelorum.* (Salzburg: Otto Müller Verlag, 1993).

Böning, Eleonore. "Jens Malte Fischer: Richard Wagner und seine Wirkung: Ohne Ekstase keine Musikzauberei." *Frankfurter Allgemeine Zeitung, May 1, 2013.*

Borchmeyer, Dieter. *Richard Wagners Antisemitismus.* (Bundeszentrale für politische Bildung, May 14, 2013).

Brüning, Eleonore. "Neues vom Giftmischer." *Frankfurter Allgemeine Zeitung,* April 7, 2013.

Büsing, Ute. "Die 120 Tage von Sodom an der Berliner Volksbühne." *RBB Kultur.* May 28, 2015.

Chamberlain, Houston Stewart. *Die Grundlagen des 19. Jahrhunderts.* (Munich: Verlag F. Bruckmann, 1942).

Chamberlain, Houston Stewart. *Richard Wagners Schriften und Lehren.* (Munich: Verlag F. Bruckmann AG, 1919).

Cohn, Norman. *Das Ringen um das tausendjährige Reich.* (Bern: Verlag Francke, 1961).

Devrient, Paul and Werner Maser, Ed. *Mein Schüler Adolf Hitler.* (Munich: Maser Werner-Verlag, 2003).

Domarus, Max, Ed. *Hitler, Reden und Proklamationen 1932-1945. Kommentiert von einem deutschen Zeitgenossen. Vol. 4.* (Mundelein, Illinois: Bolchazy-Carducci Publishers, 1988).

Döscher, Hans-Jürgen. *Reichskristallnacht. Die Novemberprogrome 1938.* (Berlin: Ullstein Verlag, 2000).

Edler, Lion. "Die so genannte Bewältigung." *Junge Freiheit,* Nov. 17, 2010.

Eisenmann, Peter. "Peter Eisenmann über Juden, Deutsche und Schuld, im Gespräch mit Chris Melzer (Deutsche Presseagentur)." *Focus,* August 10, 2012.

Fest, Joachim. *Hitler, eine Biografie.* (Berlin: Propyläen Verlag, 1998).

Feuerbach, Ludwig. *Das Wesen des Christentums.* (Ditzingen: Verlag Reclam Philipp jun., 1984).

Fischer, Jens Malte. *Richard Wagner und seine Wirkung.* (Vienna: Verlag Paul Zsolnay, 2013).

Fischer, Jens Malte Fischer. *Richard Wagners "Das Judentum in der Musik,"* (Frankfurt am Main: Insel Verlag, 2000).

Freedom Card Series I (No. 1-10). "Judaism in Opinions of the Times." (Völkische Arbeitsgemeinschaft).

Friedländer, Saul and Jörn Rüsen. *Richard Wagner im Dritten Reich. Ein Schloss Elmau Symposium.* (Munich: C. H. Beck Verlag, 2000).

Friedländer, Saul and Martin Pfeiffer. *Das Dritte Reich und die Juden: Die Jahre der Verfolgung 1933-1939. Die Jahre der Vernichtung 1939-1945.* (Munich: C. H. Beck Verlag, 2006).

Friedländer, Saul. *Nachdenken über den Holocaust.* (Munich: C. H. Beck Verlag, 2007).

Genoud, François, Ed. *Hitlers politisches Testament. Die Bormann-Diktate vom Februar und April 1945.* (Munich: A. Knaus, 1981).

George Bernard Shaw. *Ein Wagner Brevier. Kommentar zum Ring des Nibelungen.* (Berlin: Suhrkamp, 1973).

Geyer, Martin H. *Verkehrte Welt: Revolution, Inflation und Moderne, München 1914-1924.* (Göttingen: Vanderhoeck & Ruprecht, 1998).

Grimal, Pierre. *Römische Kulturgeschichte.* (Munich: Droemer/Knaur, 1961).

Grunsky, Karl. *Richard Wagner und die Juden, Vol. II.* (Munich, Deutscher Volksverlag, 1920).

Hamann, Brigitte. *Hitlers Wien, Lehrjahre eines Diktators.* (Munich: Verlag Piper, 2012).

Heer, Hannes, Jürgen Kesting and Peter Schmidt. *Verstummte Stimmen. Die Bayreuther Festspiele und die "Juden" 1876-1945.* (Berlin: Metropol Verlag, 2012).

Heinisch, Heino. *Hitlers Geiseln: Hegemonialpläne und der Holocaust.* (Vienna: Passagen Verlag, 2005).

Hiltron, Haggai. "Wagner didn't hate all Jews, just 'bad' ones, argues Israeli scholar." *Ha'aretz,* January 28, 2013.

Höbel, Wolfgang. "Meine Grundtechnik ist Zerschlagen." *Der Spiegel,* July 21, 2014.

Höbel, Wolfgang. "Tannhäuser-Skandal: Im Land der Täter und Sanitäter." *Der Spiegel,* May 10, 2013.

Höver, Ulrich. *Joseph Goebbels, ein nationaler Sozialist.* (Bonn: Verlag Bouvier, 1992).

Kalchschmid, Klaus. "Wagner und der Antisemitismus." *Süddeutsche Zeitung,* November 15, 2013.

Kampmann, Wanda. *Deutsche und Juden. Studien zur Geschichte des deutschen Judentums.* (Heidelberg: Verlag L. Schneider, 1963).

Kershaw, Ian and Klaus Kochmann. *Hitler, 1936-1945.* (Stuttgart: Deutsche Verlags-Anstalt, 2000).

Kershaw, Ian. *Wendepunkte: Schlüsselentscheidungen im Zweiten Weltkrieg.* (Munich: Pantheon, 2008).

Kiesel, Heiner. "Gauck: Aus dem Erinnern ergibt sich ein Auftrag." *Die Welt,* January 27, 2015.

Klee, Ernst. *Das Personenlexikon zum Dritten Reich: War war was vor und nach 1945.* (Frankfurt am Main: Verlag S. Fischer, 2007).

Klein, Armin. *Dossier: Öffentliche Kulturbetriebe zwischen Bildungsauftrag und Besucherorientierung.* (Bundeszentrale für politische Bildung, May 5, 2010).

Klieger, Noah. "Warum ich Wagner nicht hören will." *Der Spiegel,* July 9, 2012.

Klonovsky, Michael. "Auch du mein Apollo? Sogar in dem attischen Gott schlummert ein Nazi." *Focus,* 42/2010.

Köhler, Joachim. *Wagners Hitler, der Prophet und sein Vollstrecker.* (Munich: Verlag Blessing, 1997).

Küntzel, Matthias. "Wagner war Avantgarde – als Musiker und Antisemit." *Die Welt,* April 28, 2013.

Küntzel, Matthias. "Zum Richard-Wagner-Jahr 2013." *Die Welt am Sonntag,* April 28, 2013.

Küntzel, Matthias. "Arien für Arier? Einspruch gegen den Richard Wagner-Kult." *Die Welt am Sonntag,* April 28, 2013.

Kurbjuweit, Dirk. "Wagners Schatten." *Der Spiegel,* March 30, 2013.

Küveler, Jan. "Im Zeichen des Hakenkreuzes." *Die Welt,* August 8, 2012.

Laqueure, Walter. *Deutschland und Russland.* (Berlin: Verlag Propyläen, 1965).

Mann, Thomas. "Zu Wagners Verteidigung." *Leiden und Größe der Meister.* (Frankfurt am Main: S. Fischer Verlag, 1959).

Matthäus, Jürgen and Klaus-Michael Mallmann. *Deutsche Juden Völkermord. Der Holocaust als Geschichte und Gegenwart.* (Darmstadt: Wissenschaftliche Buchgesellschaft, 2006).

Mayer, Bernd. *Bayreuth, die letzten 50 Jahre.* (Bayreuth: Verlag Ellwanger, 1988).

Meschnig, Alexander. *Der Wille zur Bewegung: Militärischer Traum und totalitäres Programm. Eine Mentalitätsgeschichte vom Ersten Weltkrieg zum Nationalsozialismus.* (Bielefeld: transcript Verlag, 2008).

Michael Wildt. *Geschichte des Nationalsozialismus.* (Göttingen: Vandenhoeck & Ruprecht, 2007).

Möller, Barbara. "Warum Leipzig sein Richard Wagner-Denkmal nicht liebt." *Die Welt,* May 15, 2013.

Mommsen, Hans. "Der Wendepunkt zur 'Endlösung'. Die Eskalation der nationalsozialistischen Judenverfolgung" in Matthäus, Jürgen and Klaus-Michael Mallmann. *Deutsche Juden Völkermord. Der Holocaust als Geschichte und Gegenwart.* (Darmstadt: Wissenschaftliche Buchgesellschaft, 2006).

Neubauer, Emil. "Political Science 2015." *Neue Zürcher Zeitung,* December 10, 2002.

Nicosia, Francis. "Ein nützlicher Feind. Zionismus im nationalsozialistischen Deutschland 1933-1939." *Vierteljahreshefte für Zeitgeschichte,* Vol. 37, No. 3. (Munich: Institut für Zeitgeschichte, 1998).

Nierenheim, Georg. *Bayreuther Festspielführer* (Bayreuth: 1936).

Pätzold, Kurt and Manfred Weißbecker. *Stufen zum Galgen: Lebenswege vor den Nürnberger Urteilen.* (Berlin: Militzke Verlag, 2004).

Phelps, R. H. *Dokumentation: Hitlers "grundlegende" Rede über den Antisemitismus.* (Stuttgart: Deutsche Verlags-Anstalt, 1968).

Piper, Ernst. *Alfred Rosenberg, Hitlers Chefideologe.* (Munich: Verlag Karl Blessing/C. Bertelsmann, Random House, 2005).

Plöckinger, Othmar. *Geschichte eines Buches: Adolf Hitler: "Mein Kampf": 1922-1945.* (Munich: Oldenbourg Verlag, 2006).

Prestel, Peter and Rudolf Sporrer. "Hitlers Ordensburgen." 3sat, August 28, 2009.

Pretzsch, Paul. *Cosima Wagner und Houston Stewart Chamberlain im Briefwechsel, 1888-1908.* (Leipzig: Verlag Philipp Reclam jun., 1934).

Reiter, Raymond. *Hitlers Geheimpolitik.* (Berlin/Munich: Verlag Peter Lang, 2008).

Reuth, Ralf G. Goebbels. (Munich/Zürich: Piper Verlag, 1990).

Rose, Paul Lawrence. *Richard Wagner und der Antisemitismus.* (Zurich: Pendo Verlag, 1999).

Rosenberg, Alfred. *Letzte Aufzeichnungen.* (Göttingen: Plesse-Verlag, 1955.)

Rosenberg, Alfred. *Die Protokolle der Weisen von Zion und die jüdische Weltpolitik.* (München: Deutscher Volksverlag, 1933).

Rosenberg, Alfred. *Das Parteiprogramm. Wesen, Grundsätze und Ziele der NSDAP.* (Munich: Zentralverlag des NSDAP, 1941).

Rosenberg, Alfred. *Der Mythos des 20. Jahrhunderts.* (Munich: Deutscher Taschenbuchverlag, 1988).

Rosenberg, Alfred. *Letzte Aufzeichnungen: Nürnberg 1945/46.* (Uelzen: *Jomsburg Verlag,* 1996).

Ross, Alex. "The Case for Wagner in Israel." Culture Desk, *The New Yorker,* Sept. 25, 2012.

Schiff, András. "Was zum Teufel ist mit dem deutschen Theater los?" *Neue Züricher Zeitung,* October 27, 2014.

Schönburg, Alexander von. "Blutiger Sadomaso-Sex auf der Bühne," *Bild,* May 28, 2015.

Sembritzki, Katja. "Schützenjäger, Antisemit, begnadeter Komponist. Wagners dunkle Flecken bleiben." ntv.de, May 22, 2013.

Smith, Adam and Laurence Winant Dickey. *Inquiry into the Nature and Causes of the Wealth of Nations.* (Cambridge: Hackett Publishing Co., Inc., 1993).

Spahn, Claus. "Was deutsch und echt." *Die Zeit,* April 16, 1998.

Steinacker, Olaf. "Der heftig kritisierte Tannhäuser wird abgesetzt." *Westdeutsche Zeitung,* May 8, 2013.

Sternfeld, Richard. *Richard Wagner und die Bayreuther Bühnenfestspiele,* Vol. 2. (Berlin: Verlag Deutsche Bücherei, 1906).

Sucher, Bernd C. *Takt 2.* (Munich: Bayerische Staatsoper, 2003).

Thacker, Toby. *Joseph Goebbels: Life and Death.* (London/New York: Palgrave Macmillan Basingstoke, 2009).

Tyrell, Albrecht. *Führer befiehl ... Selbstzeugnisse aus der Kampfzeit der NSDAP.* (Bindlach: Verlag Gondrom, 1991).

Vaget, Hans R. *Im Schatten Wagners: Thomas Mann über Richard Wagner.* (Frankfurt am Main: S. Fischer Verlag, 2010).

Vinogradov, V. K. and J. F. Ponogyi. *Hitler's Death: Russia's Last Great Secret from the Files of the KGB.* (London: Chaucer Press, 2005).

Völkischer Beobachter, July 11, 1936.

Wagner, Cosima, Martin Gregor-Martin and Dietrich Mack, *Tagebücher, Vol. 4 (1881-1883).* (Munich: Piper Verlag, 1982).

Wagner, Gottfried and Abraham J. Peck. *Unsere Stunde Null: Deutsche und Juden nach 1945: Familiengeschichte, Holocaust und Neubeginn. Historische Memoiren.* (Vienna: Böhlau Verlag, 2006).

Wagner, Gottfried. *Du sollst keine anderen Götter haben neben mir: Richard Wagner – Ein Minenfeld.* (Berlin: Propyläen Verlag, 2013).

Wagner, Richard. "Das Wiener Hof-Operntheater." *Der Botschafter,* Vienna, 1863.

Walter, Dirk. *Antisemitische Kriminalität und Judenfeindschaft in der Weimarer Republik.* (Bonn: Verlag J.H.W. Dietz, 1999).

Wapnewsky, Peter. *Richard Wagner, Die Szene und ihr Meister.* (Munich: Verlag C.H. Beck, 1978)

Wehler, Hans-Ulrich. *Der Nationalsozialismus: Bewegung, Führerschaft, Verbrechen 1919-1945.* (Munich: Verlag C. H. Beck, 2009).

Wehler, Hans-Ulrich. *Deutsche Gesellschaftsgeschichte, Vol. 4.* (Munich: C. H. Beck Verlag, 2008).

Weikl, Bernd and Peter Bendixen. *Freispruch für Richard Wagner?* (Leipzig: Universitätsverlag Leipzig, 2012).

Weiner, Marc A. *Antisemitische Fantasien.* (Berlin: Henschel Verlag, 2000).

Weiss, Hermann. *Biografisches Lexikon zum Dritten Reich.* (Frankfurt am Main: S. Fischer, 1998).

Wenzel, Mario. "Germanische Herrenrasse," in Wolfgang Benz, Ed., *Handbuch des Antisemitismus. Judenfeindschaft in Geschichte und Gegenwart,* Vol. 3. (Berlin: Verlag De Gryteer/Saur, 2010).

Wiggerhaus, Renate. Ulrike Helmer, Ed. *Malwida Meysenbug, Memoiren einer Idealistin.* (Königstein: Edition Klassikerinnen, 1998).

Wistrich, Robert and Hermann Weiss. *Wer war wer im Dritten Reich. Anhänger, Mitläufer, Gegner aus Politik, Wirtschaft, Militär, Kunst und Wissenschaft.* (Munich: Fischer Verlag, 1983).

Witte, Peter, Michael Wildt and Martin Voigt. *Der Dienstkalender Heinrich Himmlers.* (Konstanz: Verlag Christians, 1999).

Wolfgang Schreiber. "Gottfried Wagner: Du sollst keine anderen Götter haben neben mir." *Süddeutsche Zeitung,* April 20, 2013.

Zehnpfennig, Barbara. *Hitlers Mein Kampf: Eine Interpretation.* (Hamburg/Munich: Wilhelm Fink Verlag, 2006).

Zelle, Karl-Günter. "Joseph Goebbels: Aussen- und Innenansichten eines Propagandisten." (Berlin: AGGB - Arbeitsgemeinschaft der Gedenkstätten und Bibliotheken, 2010).

Zelle, Karl-Günter. *Hitlers zweifelnde Elite: Goebbels – Göring – Himmler – Speer.* (Paderborn: Schöningh Verlag, 2010).

Biography

Born in Vienna in 1942, Bernd Weikl spent his early childhood in his father's Bavarian homeland in the mountains bridging Germany and Czechoslovakia with his mother, who was originally from Hungary. His father had been drafted into the German army and returned home from France when the war ended. In 1952, Bernd moved to Mainz with his family and studied economics and voice there in the early 1960s before attending the Hannover Musikhochschule as of 1965.

In the course of his career as a leading operatic baritone, Bernd Weikl amassed a repertoire of over 120 roles, performing the Italian, French and Russian repertoire, as well as the major Strauss and Wagner works, including his signature role, Hans Sachs in *Die Meistersinger von Nürnberg*, at all of the world's principal opera houses.

Alongside his international opera and concert activities, Bernd Weikl has established a reputation as a writer and panelist in prominent forums. His interests are as broad as his repertoire and comprise mainly philosophical, social, sociological and economic issues. Weikl integrates these issues into comprehensive conceptual models, with a particular focus on the role of the artist in the present-day conflict between culture and commerce.